Moro East

Moro East

SAM AND SAM CLARK

Photographs by Toby Glanville

Ebury Press
LONDON

NOTE: All spoon measures are level unless otherwise specified.

5 7 9 10 8 6 4

Published in 2007 by Ebury Press, an imprint of Ebury Publishing

Ebury Publishing is a division of the Random House Group

The Random House Group Limited Reg. No. 954009

Addresses for companies within the Random House Group can be found at www.randomhouse.co.uk

A CIP catalogue record for this book is available from the British Library

The Random House Group makes every effort to ensure that the papers used in our books are made from trees that have been legally sourced from well-managed and credibly certified forests. Our paper procurement policy can be found on www.randomhouse.co.uk

Design and art direction: Caz Hildebrand

Photography: Toby Glanville

Editor: Jane Middleton

Printed and bound in Italy by Graphicon SRL

ISBN: 978 0 09191 777 7

To buy books by your favourite authors and register for offers visit www.rbooks.co.uk

Contents

Introduction

We needed courage to find our allotment for the first time. The vast area east of Victoria Park has a dusty bleakness, unusual for London. If bicycling there, we have to keep away from the kerb to avoid broken glass and rusty metal. The smell of burnt cow hair from the meat processing plant adds to the atmosphere. The only clue that there is any gardening life in the area is the wild rocket pushing out of the cracks in the pavement. Beside the bus depot, out of sight of the road, is a barbed rusty gate, behind which things change dramatically.

You can't help but gasp when you open the gate and find yourself standing at the foot of a 70-metre bridge high over the river, looking across to a bank of wild plums, elderflower and blackberries. There is not a building in sight, just the odd proud shed. Here are the land and the community that have been so important to us over the past seven years.

When we think of our first season on the allotment, we are reminded of cooking for friends and family when we were young. Bright-eyed, eager, we spent vast amounts of time preparing food, with very mixed results. In our modern lives, whether growing our own vegetables or cooking elaborate meals, it just doesn't add up. It's irrational. But why does it give us so much damn pleasure?

The first person we met was our neighbour Hassan: kind Mr Charisma, who was to become our friend and

mentor. He introduced us to other people on the allotment – Cypriots, Kurds and Turks. We soon realised that we were among special people who thought differently about growing and could teach us much about cooking too. Our eyes were opened to things such as frying green tomatoes, cooking artichoke leaves, braising wild poppy leaves, and much more. The Eastern Mediterranean was alive in Hackney Wick.

Last year our crops suffered an unusual amount of damage from rabbits. We were puzzled as to the reason, but then it clicked: the Olympics were coming. Like a scene from *Watership Down*, the diggers were encroaching and the rabbits were escaping and settling where they could. By the time you read this book our century-old allotment will have been replaced by a hockey stadium, we will have been moved on, and after a struggle (see Acknowledgements) we have been granted an alternative site.

So now we must start afresh, scratching around in a new patch of earth. We feel sure that with a handful of seeds and a healthy dose of optimism we can regain our paradise.

Soups

Jamón broth with broad beans, asparagus and poached egg

Spring is one of the most exciting times of the year on the allotment, as we watch the sparse winter beds come to life with early crops such as broad beans and asparagus. We also like to harvest tender pea shoots, shredding a couple of handfuls and adding them to this soup with the broad beans. Later in the summer, the best vegetables to use are thinly sliced artichoke hearts and peas, or indeed any late broad beans. The combination of jamón, broad beans and mint is so classically Spanish, with strong echoes of *sopa de ajo* – Castilla-La Mancha's most famous garlic broth.

Serves 4

170g jamón serrano, finely
    shredded with a sharp knife
1.4 litres good light chicken stock
2 teaspoons fresh thyme leaves
3 tablespoons fino sherry
150g podded young broad beans
1 bunch of green asparagus spears
4 organic eggs

4 slices of rustic bread (sourdough
    or ciabatta)
1 garlic clove, peeled, and some good
    extra virgin olive oil for the toast
1 tablespoon finely chopped
    fresh mint
a sprinkling of sweet paprika,
    smoked or unsmoked

Gently simmer 150g of the jamón in the stock with the thyme for 15 minutes or until you can taste its sweet saltiness, skimming occasionally. Remove the jamón with a slotted spoon and discard, then add the fino sherry and season to taste with salt and pepper. This can be done a little in advance, if you like.

Meanwhile, fill a medium saucepan with unsalted water and place over a high heat. When it is boiling, add the broad beans and simmer for 2–3 minutes, until tender. Drain in a colander and refresh under cold water. Peel any beans larger than your thumbnail, as these will have a tough outer skin.

To prepare the asparagus, snap the woody stems off at the base, halve them lengthways if they are thick, and slice in 1cm lengths.

About 5 minutes before you are ready to serve, place the broth over the heat. When it is gently simmering, add the asparagus and cook for a minute before poaching the eggs in the broth. To do this, break each egg into a bowl and slide it into the soup. While they are poaching, toast the bread, then rub with the clove of garlic and drizzle liberally with the oil.

When the egg whites are almost set, add the drained broad beans to the broth to heat through, plus the remaining shredded jamón and the mint. Taste once more for seasoning. Serve immediately, with the toasted bread and a sprinkling of paprika.

Clockwise from the top: poppy leaves, nettle tops, mallow leaves, sorrel, chick-weed and wild rocket. Self-seeded and wild around the allotment, May 2007.

Wanderer's soup

This recipe is based on a velvety chicken and potato broth which provides a lovely backdrop for the fruits of foraging. When one hunts for greens, it is quite unusual to find large quantities of any one species – it is easier to get a mixture of two or three. In a city park or by a canal, we would probably pick chickweed, mallow and dandelion. On a country walk we might find sorrel, young nettle tops, wild garlic and ground elder and, self-seeded on the allotment, fennel, nasturtium leaves, wild rocket, young poppy leaves, borage or young courgette leaves. Go on, give it a go – foraging is surprisingly addictive.

Serves 4

50g unsalted butter

3 tablespoons olive oil

1 large or 2 medium onions, finely
　　chopped

3 medium potatoes (about 600g),
　　peeled and thinly sliced

3 garlic cloves, chopped

3 fresh bay leaves

800ml light chicken stock

a few gratings of nutmeg

4 handfuls (about 200g) of foraged
　　greens (or a mixture of sorrel,
　　rocket, dandelion and parsley),
　　washed and finely chopped

150g cooking chorizo, diced
　　small

In a large saucepan, melt the butter in 2 tablespoons of the oil over a medium-high heat. Soften the onions with a pinch of salt for 15–20 minutes, stirring occasionally, until golden. Turn down the heat to medium-low and stir in the potatoes, garlic, bay leaves and another pinch of salt. Put a lid on and cook gently, stirring often so the potatoes do not stick, for 25 minutes or until the potatoes are tender. Add the stock and nutmeg, bring to the boil and simmer for 5–10 minutes. Remove the bay leaves, double-check the potatoes are cooked and remove from the heat. Whizz with a handheld blender (or in a food processor) until very smooth. Up to this point, all stages can be done ahead of time.

When you are ready to serve, reheat the soup if necessary and stir in your greens. Bring back to the boil and immediately remove from the heat. Meanwhile, fry the chorizo in the remaining oil in a small pan until well coloured, cooked through, and crisp in parts. Check the soup for seasoning and serve with the chorizo and its delicious red oil spooned on top.

Courgette and yoghurt soup

This soup can be served hot or, on a warm day, chilled. If you are growing courgettes, then you may have a number of courgette flowers at your disposal. Remove the stalk and stamen of the male flowers (no fruit), shred the flowers carefully and stir in at the end with the mint.

Serves 4

400g good-quality Greek yoghurt,
    such as Total
1 egg yolk
$1/2$ tablespoon cornflour (or plain
    flour)
750ml chicken or vegetable stock
1.5kg courgettes, topped and tailed,
    sliced into thin rounds
1 teaspoon fine sea salt
50g unsalted butter

1 tablespoon olive oil
2 garlic cloves, thinly sliced
2 tablespoons roughly chopped
    fresh mint
4 male courgette flowers, petals only,
    chopped (optional)
$1/2$ teaspoon dried Turkish (mild)
    chilli flakes
$1/2$ teaspoon dried mint (optional)

Caramelised butter
50g unsalted butter

To caramelise the butter, place it in a small saucepan over the lowest possible heat. As the butter melts, the whey will separate out. Continue to heat gently, stirring occasionally, until the white bits turn golden brown. This gives the butter a wonderfully nutty, caramelised aroma, but be careful the bits do not get too dark, as they will burn easily. Remove from the heat and set aside.

In a large bowl, whisk the yoghurt with the egg yolk and cornflour until smooth. This will stabilise the yoghurt so it will not split when heated. Now stir in all the stock to thin it and set aside.

Place the courgette slices in a colander and toss evenly with the salt. Leave them to sit for at least 10 minutes over a draining board or sink, then pat dry with kitchen paper.

In a large saucepan, melt the butter with the olive oil over a medium heat. Stir in the courgettes, garlic and half the fresh mint and cook for 30–40 minutes, stirring occasionally, until the courgettes are soft and sweet and reduced in volume by about half. At this point you can decide how much texture you'd like your soup to have. We mash about half the courgettes in the saucepan with a potato masher, which leaves a lightly textured soup. Stir the yoghurt/stock into the courgettes and bring to a gentle simmer (if you used flour rather than cornflour, let it simmer for a minute to get rid of any starchiness). Season with salt and pepper. Stir through the remaining fresh mint and the courgette flowers, if using. Serve each bowl of soup with some caramelised butter and a sprinkling of dried chilli and mint, if using, on top.

Beetroot gazpacho

At first we were slightly wary of this variation of a classic gazpacho, as it seemed a bit trendy and untraditional. But once you try it, the lushness of the colour and sweetness of the taste will bring joy to even the most sceptical palate. Sometimes we also like to serve it in a glass to show off its dazzling colour and to make a change from the ubiquitous soup bowl.

Beetroot are ready in late summer, just as the last of your tomatoes are ripe and at their best.

Serves 4

750g sweet tomatoes, halved

350g raw beetroot, peeled and chopped into small pieces

1 green pepper, seeded, cored and sliced

$^3/_4$ large cucumber, peeled and sliced

2 rounded dessertspoons finely grated onion

2 garlic cloves, crushed to a paste with a pinch of salt

2 handfuls of dry white bread, crusts removed, roughly crumbled

3 dessertspoons good-quality red wine vinegar or sherry vinegar

4 dessertspoons extra virgin olive oil, plus an extra drizzle at the end

Using a blender or food processor, purée all the vegetables with the garlic and bread until as smooth as possible, letting the machine run for several minutes. Now pass three-quarters of the mixture through a fine sieve to give a smoother texture, pushing it down with the back of a ladle. Combine the strained and unstrained parts in a bowl and finish by seasoning the soup with the vinegar, oil and some salt and black pepper. Put it in the fridge for a couple of hours to chill, then check the seasoning once again before serving with an extra drizzle of olive oil on top.

Cacik

This ancient cold soup comes from the Eastern Mediterranean, Turkey in particular, and is perfect for a hot summer's day. The combination of cucumber, yoghurt and mint is the ultimate in cooling flavours.

Our cucumbers were particularly ugly this year, due to drought and neglect. When used in this soup, however, they tasted divine and all their physical imperfections were forgiven.

Serves 4–5

1kg cucumbers (about 2 large ones), partly peeled and coarsely grated

2 tablespoons pine nuts

2 tablespoons sunflower, olive or vegetable oil

500g good-quality Greek yoghurt, such as Total

2 garlic cloves, crushed with 1 teaspoon of salt

2 tablespoons chopped fresh mint

500ml milk

2 tablespoons olive oil, plus an extra drizzle at the end

lemon juice to taste – a good squeeze

2 dessertspoons currants or small raisins, soaked in hot water until plump

$1/2$ teaspoon dried mint (optional)

Toss the grated cucumber with a good pinch of fine sea salt and leave in a colander for 10 minutes. Meanwhile, gently fry the pine nuts in the oil in a small pan until they begin to colour. Drain and place on kitchen paper to cool. Squeeze the cucumber to remove as much liquid as possible. Place in a large bowl with the yoghurt, garlic, fresh mint, milk, olive oil and lemon juice and mix well. Season with salt and freshly ground black pepper, then put in the fridge to chill. Serve with the plumped currants or raisins, pine nuts and dried mint, if using, on top of each bowl, plus a drizzle of olive oil.

Hassan's celery and white bean soup with tomato and caraway

We have been lucky enough to savour this soup cooked by our allotment neighbour, Hassan, on more than one occasion. It is as good and wholesome as any minestrone but eternally satisfying when made with produce plucked from the patch that lies in front of his shed (white beans excepted). Accompanied by Turkish bread, spring onions and oily black olives, this steaming soup revives the soul.

Celery tends to be a background flavour for most soups and stews, so it is refreshing to have a recipe that uses it as a main ingredient, and every bit is included, leaves and all. The caraway is our addition to Hassan's recipe and is optional. Depending on the season, try adding other vegetables, such as courgettes, fennel, sorrel or chard.

Serves 4–6

250g dried cannellini beans, soaked in cold water overnight (or 650g cooked beans – drained weight)

10 tablespoons (150ml) olive oil

1 large head of celery with leaves, trimmed of roots, then sliced across in 2cm chunks

8 spring onions, green tops included, sliced into 1cm rounds

4 garlic cloves, thinly sliced

1 teaspoon caraway seeds, lightly crushed (optional)

500g flavoursome tomatoes, blanched, peeled and seeded, then roughly chopped

1 teaspoon celery salt (see note, opposite)

To serve

extra virgin olive oil

a squeeze of lemon juice

4–6 whole spring onions, trimmed

a small bunch of any or all of the following: rocket, sorrel and radish

a small bowl of oily black olives

Turkish bread, if possible

Drain the soaked beans and place in a saucepan with plenty of fresh water. Bring to the boil and simmer gently for approximately 1 hour or until tender, skimming off any scum and topping up the water as necessary. Season with salt and set aside.

Meanwhile, place a large saucepan over a medium to high heat and add 6 tablespoons of the olive oil. When it is hot, add the celery and cook for 10 minutes, stirring often. Now add the spring onions, garlic, caraway, if using, and a good pinch of salt. Cook for 10–15 minutes, stirring every now and then, until the vegetables are soft and beginning to caramelise. Add the tomatoes and half the celery salt and cook for a further 5 minutes. Drain the beans, reserving 250ml of their cooking liquor, and stir them into the pan with the reserved liquor or water and the remaining 4 tablespoons of olive oil. Bring to a simmer, season with salt, if needed, and pepper and cook for another 5 minutes. Check the seasoning once more.

Serve with a generous drizzle of olive oil, a squeeze of lemon and the remaining celery salt on top. Eat with alternate mouthfuls of spring onions, greens, black olives and bread, as these accompaniments are very much part of the experience.

Note

To make your own celery salt, place a handful of green celery leaves on a baking tray and dry in a low-medium oven, moving them around until completely dry but not scorched. Crumble to a powder with your fingers, removing any long veins, and mix with equal parts (by eye) of Maldon salt.

Tomato soup with cumin and figs

This soup is based on a recipe from Fra Juan's restaurant in the monastery of Guadalupe. It is strictly a summer dish, an interesting Spanish twist on a classic tomato soup. While serving this soup at the restaurant, a waiter over-heard a customer say it was the best tomato soup she had ever had. Of course, it was a moment when the ingredients did shine. It was at the beginning of August, after a heatwave, and British tomatoes tasted as good as they get. The allotment figs were superb, too. It's a thrill to find recipes that have been cooked for hundreds of years, but in the end this means nothing unless the ingredients are at their peak.

Serves 4

6 tablespoons olive oil

1 medium onion, chopped

1 green pepper, chopped

3 garlic cloves, chopped

$2^1/_2$ teaspoons cumin seeds, lightly toasted in a pan, then crushed

400g tin of chopped plum tomatoes, drained of juice

100g dried figs, chopped

1kg flavourful tomatoes, roughly sliced

150–300ml water

a little caster sugar (optional)

5 or 6 ripe, plump fresh figs, finely diced

a drizzle of extra virgin olive oil, to serve

Heat the olive oil in a saucepan over a medium heat, add the onion and green pepper with a good pinch of salt and cook gently for 15–20 minutes, stirring occasionally, until softened. Add the garlic and continue cooking until sweet and golden brown. Add two-thirds of the cumin and cook for 1 minute more. Now add the tinned tomatoes and dried figs and simmer gently, uncovered, for 50–60 minutes, stirring now and then. When the mixture is rich and concen-trated, put in the fresh tomatoes and increase the heat slightly, then simmer for 15 minutes more. With a handheld blender, whizz until smooth, then pour in enough of the water to achieve a consistency like double cream. Season well with salt, pepper and sugar if necessary.

   Stir half the fresh figs through the soup and use the rest to garnish each portion in the bowl, along with the remaining cumin and a drizzle of extra virgin olive oil.

Cauliflower and cumin soup

The inspiration for this soup came to us in a high mountain village in the Alpujarras in Andalucía as we chatted with a fellow traveller into the small hours of the morning. She described a soup she'd eaten on holiday in Zanzibar – and here it is now with some variations. Of course it's always tempting, when a customer asks us where it comes from, to embark on a mythical journey involving camel routes and coconuts swollen by the flooding of the Nile.

The soup is very subtly flavoured with coconut, and the addition of chilli butter and pine nuts is just to play around with the texture and taste. Cauliflower crops three times a year, in the summer, autumn and winter, and so is an all-year-round vegetable on the allotment.

Serves 4–5

2 tablespoons olive oil

2 tablespoons pine nuts

60g unsalted butter

2 medium onions, finely chopped

$2^1/_2$ teaspoons cumin seeds

3 garlic cloves, chopped

$^1/_2$ teaspoon ground cinnamon

1 very large or 2 medium
   cauliflowers (about 1.5kg), core
   removed, roughly chopped

270ml tinned coconut milk

400ml vegetable stock (or water)

200ml milk

Caramelised chilli butter

60g unsalted butter

$^1/_2$ teaspoon hot paprika (unsmoked)
   or $^1/_3$ teaspoon chilli powder

Caramelise the butter as described on page 6, adding the paprika or chilli at the end.

Put the olive oil and pine nuts in a large saucepan, at least 25cm wide. Fry over a medium heat, stirring all the time, until the pine nuts just start to colour. Remove with a slotted spoon and put to one side. Put the butter in the pan and when it foams, add the onions and a pinch of salt. Fry over a medium heat for 20–30 minutes, stirring often, until golden. Meanwhile, roast the cumin seeds in a small frying pan over a medium heat, stirring all the time, until they have begun to brown – this takes just a minute or two. Crush them in a mortar and pestle (one of the most evocative and pleasurable smells is that of crushing warm, browned cumin).

Add the garlic, cumin and cinnamon to the onions and cook for a further 5 minutes. Stir in the cauliflower and some salt and pepper. Put a lid on and steam for 20 minutes, stirring once or twice. Take off the lid and mash coarsely with a potato masher. Continue to cook with the lid off for 20 minutes, mashing every now and then. Pour in the coconut milk, stock, and milk. Simmer for 10 minutes, until the cauliflower is completely soft, then remove from the heat and blend the soup with a hand blender until almost smooth. Check the final seasoning and serve in bowls, with a drizzle of warmed chilli butter and the pine nuts on top.

Mansaf

This Jordanian yoghurt and saffron broth is traditionally made with braised lamb. Our version with spiced kifta meatballs is quicker, lighter and just as delicious. We were shown this soup by one of our chefs, Nader, and ever since it has been a favourite.

Serves 4

80g unsalted butter
1 large onion, finely chopped (about
    200g)
30g flaked almonds
50g pine nuts
400g jar of cooked chickpeas, drained
2 good pinches of saffron (about 40
    strands in each pinch), soaked in
    2 tablespoons boiling water

800ml good chicken stock, hot
1 egg yolk
1 teaspoon cornflour or plain flour
250g good-quality Greek yoghurt,
    such as Total
2 tablespoons roughly chopped
    flat-leaf parsley

Kifta

200g minced lamb
50g crustless white bread, moistened
    with 2 tablespoons milk
1 garlic clove, crushed to a paste
    with a pinch of salt

1 teaspoon ground cumin
1 teaspoon sweet paprika
3 tablespoons olive oil

For the kifta, combine the lamb, bread, garlic, spices and some salt and pepper in a food processor and blend until just coming together. Roll into 35–40 hazelnut-sized meatballs, then leave in the fridge for half an hour, if time allows. Heat the oil in a wide, heavy saucepan until very hot, then add the meatballs and brown lightly, stirring ever so gently. Remove the meatballs and place on kitchen paper to absorb excess oil. Discard the oil in the pan but re-use the pan for the soup.

Add the butter to the still-hot pan, let it foam, then add the onion and a pinch of salt. Scrape the bottom of the pan with a wooden spoon to release any sticking fragments of lamb. Let the onion soften for about 20 minutes, then add the almonds and pine nuts. Cook for 10–20 minutes, stirring

constantly to ensure that the onions and nuts cook beautifully and do not burn. Now add the meatballs and chickpeas and cook for 5 minutes more. Add the saffron-infused water and the hot stock and bring to the boil. While the soup is coming up to temperature, whisk the egg yolk and cornflour into the yoghurt to stabilise it. Once boiling, stir a couple of ladlefuls of the hot soup into the yoghurt mixture, then add it all back to the pan and bring to a simmer for another minute or so. Stir in the parsley, season with salt and pepper and serve hot.

Roast pumpkin soup with cinnamon

We grow a variety of squash and pumpkin on the allotment, partly because we love cooking with them and partly because, given their sprawling nature, they take up a lot of room. Our plot is bigger than we need and so the more they grow, the more they trail their leaves, stalks and fruit over a wide area. This year we grew pumpkins for Halloween as well as for cooking, but unfortunately the whole crop was hollowed out by rabbits before the children could get to them (see the photograph on page 190).

The choice of pumpkin or squash is key to the flavour of this soup and we have recently taken to using a mix – kabocha for starchiness, and butternut, hubbard or crown prince for sweetness. We roast the pumpkin to intensify its flavour.

Serves 4

600g peeled and seeded pumpkin or
    squash (equivalent to about 1kg
    unprepared pumpkin), cut into
    3cm cubes
6 tablespoons olive oil
1 medium onion, thinly sliced across
    the grain
2 garlic cloves, thinly sliced
$1/2$ teaspoon freshly ground cinnamon
a pinch of crushed dried chilli

1 medium potato (about 150g),
    peeled and cut into 2cm cubes
1 litre vegetable (or chicken) stock,
    preferably hot
1 medium bunch (about 40g) of
    coriander, coarsely chopped
1–2 teaspoons caster sugar
    (optional, depending on the
    sweetness of the pumpkin)

To serve
50g unsalted butter
30g pine nuts
$1/2$ teaspoon ground cinnamon

100g good-quality Greek yoghurt,
    such as Total, thinned with
    1 tablespoon milk
$1/4$ garlic clove, crushed to a paste
    with a pinch of salt

Preheat the oven to 220°C/425°F/Gas 7.

Toss the pumpkin with 2 tablespoons of the olive oil, a good pinch of salt and some black pepper and spread it out in a roasting tin. Roast for about an hour, until very soft and starting to colour.

About 20 minutes before the pumpkin is ready, heat the remaining oil in a large saucepan over a medium heat. Add the onion and a pinch of salt and cook for about 15 minutes, stirring occasionally, until the onion begins to turn golden. Now add the garlic, cinnamon and chilli. Fry for another minute to release their flavour, then add the potato and a little salt and pepper. Cook for 5 minutes more, taking care that the garlic doesn't burn, then add the roasted pumpkin and the stock and bring to a gentle simmer. Cook for 20 minutes or until the potato is soft.

Meanwhile, prepare the garnishes. Melt the butter in your smallest pan, add the pine nuts and cinnamon and fry gently until the butter begins to caramelise and foam and the pine nuts are starting to turn a very pale brown. Scrape the bottom of the pan to release any bits that are stuck and pour the pine nuts and butter into a cool bowl to stop the cooking. In another bowl, season the yoghurt with the crushed garlic and some salt and pepper.

With a handheld blender or in a food processor, blend the soup until smooth. Return it to the pan, stir in the chopped coriander and check for seasoning. If the soup is not sweet enough, add a little sugar. Serve with the seasoned yoghurt, warm brown butter and pine nuts on top.

Almond and fennel soup
with scallops

In this soup, the perfumed flavours of the fennel and blanched almonds combine well with the tastes of the sea and the nutty crunch of roasted almonds. For extra colour and flavour, use the tops of Florentine fennel or sprigs of fennel herb, which seeds itself in many gardens and allotments.

We struggled to make this soup taste right. We liked the combination of almonds and fennel but the flavours were a bit too ethereal. It was our tester, Jacob, who came up with the idea of adding the scallops and along with the fino sherry, it transformed the soup into something quite special. Thank you, Jacob!

Serves 4

5 tablespoons olive oil

1 medium onion, finely chopped

4–5 fennel bulbs (1kg trimmed
weight), finely chopped

2 fresh bay leaves

3 garlic cloves, chopped

100g blanched almonds, roasted in
a low oven until golden

1 litre light fish stock, preferably hot

To serve

6 large scallops

2 tablespoons olive oil, plus an
extra drizzle

50g almonds, thinly sliced

a small bunch (about 15g) of young
fennel tops (or flat–leaf parsley),
finely chopped

2 tablespoons fino sherry

Heat the olive oil in a saucepan, add the onion with a good pinch of salt and soften over a medium heat for 15 minutes, stirring occasionally. Add the fennel, bay and garlic and cook for 30 minutes, still stirring every now and then, until the fennel is very soft.

Meanwhile, prepare the garnishes. Remove the corals from the scallops, set aside and discard the tough 'feet'. Lightly season the scallops with salt and pepper. Set a frying pan over a high heat and when hot, add the oil, closely followed by the scallops. Sear until golden brown on both sides but not cooked through. Add the corals for a couple of seconds (watch out – they pop and spit). Transfer the scallops and corals to a cool plate and chill in the fridge before dicing them finely. Toast the sliced almonds in a moderate oven until golden and let them cool. Mix the scallops and almonds with half the chopped fennel tops.

Now grind the whole almonds in a food processor until as fine as possible – about 5 long minutes! Dislodge any almonds stuck to the side, add 1 tablespoon of the stock and turn the machine on once more. Purée for a couple of minutes more to release the almond oils. Gradually add some more of the stock to the almonds to make an emulsified liquid. Add to the fennel mix along with the rest of the stock. Bring to the boil and check for seasoning. Just before serving, stir in the fino sherry and the remaining fennel tops. Put some of the scallop/almond mixture at the bottom of each bowl, ladle over the soup, and finish with the remaining scallop mixture on top and a drizzle of olive oil.

Fava bean soup with morcilla

Dried fava beans are dried peeled broad beans. They are hard to get hold of if you don't have access to a Turkish or Middle Eastern grocer. In mid-summer you are more likely to find huge and floury fresh broad beans in your greengrocer's or, if you have a glut, in your garden or allotment. Peel them and use as you would dried, but bear in mind that you will need about double the weight when using podded and peeled fresh beans, and they will take only a few minutes to become soft and tender.

Serves 4

200g dried peeled fava beans

2 litres water

2 fresh bay leaves

1 teaspoon fennel seeds

2 cloves

5 tablespoons olive oil

350g morcilla (or black pudding), sliced into rounds

100g cooking chorizo, finely diced

4 medium leeks, trimmed and thinly sliced

3 garlic cloves, chopped

2 medium potatoes (about 400g), peeled and thinly sliced

1 teaspoon finely chopped fresh rosemary

1 tablespoon roughly chopped fresh flat-leaf parsley

Rinse the beans and place in a large saucepan. Add the water and bring to a simmer, skimming off any scum. Add the bay leaves, fennel seeds and cloves and cook for 30–40 minutes, until the beans are soft. Drain, reserving the liquid.

Meanwhile, in another saucepan, heat the olive oil over a high heat, then add the morcilla and fry until it starts to crisp. Lift the morcilla out of the pan with a slotted spoon, chop roughly and keep to one side. Now add the chorizo and fry for 2–4 minutes, until it begins to colour. Add the leeks and garlic, season with salt and pepper, and cook over a medium heat for 15 minutes, until soft and sweet. Stir in the potatoes and rosemary, reduce the heat to low and cover with a lid. Cook gently for 20–25 minutes, stirring every now and then. When the potatoes are soft, add the beans and mash roughly with a potato masher.

Stir in 600–700ml of the cooking liquid from the beans, mash until almost smooth, then add the parsley and half of the morcilla. Bring to the boil, check for seasoning and serve with the remaining morcilla on top.

Spiced lamb soup

This Tunisian soup is based on a recipe in Paula Wolfert's wonderful book, *Mediterranean Cooking* (HarperCollins, 1994), where sliced shin of veal is used. We use lamb shanks in a penny-pinching sort of way, as we always have an abundance after preparing legs of lamb for the charcoal grill.

The soup has a fascinating spice mix, and though it might not be easy to buy aniseed we urge you to do so even though it takes a while to get through in any kitchen. To use up a surplus, try pouring boiling water over some to make an excellent herbal tea. We sometimes serve this hearty soup as a stew, accompanied by a salad or vegetables: just double the quantities, and don't shred the meat.

A note about grinding spices

If you love your spice, always grind whole spices freshly each time you use them. We are huge fans of the mortar and pestle, especially for crushing garlic or small quantities of spices, but we also use a coffee grinder for larger quantities and harder-to-grind spices such as cinnamon. Both items are inexpensive, and investing in either means you can have freshly ground spices at your fingertips in a matter of seconds. Pre-ground spices go stale very quickly, which does make a big difference to the flavours.

Serves 4

$1/2$ heaped teaspoon whole aniseed

$1/2$ heaped teaspoon coriander seeds

3 whole cloves

$1/2$ teaspoon caraway seeds

4 tablespoons olive oil

2 medium lamb shanks off the bone,
    or a neck of lamb in 3 pieces
    (600g, bone-in)

2 garlic cloves, chopped

$1/2$ rounded teaspoon turmeric

$1/2$ teaspoon ground black pepper

$1/2$ teaspoon ground cinnamon

$3/4$ teaspoon smoked hot paprika

8 celery sticks, very finely chopped
    by hand or in a food processor

1 small bunch (about 20g) of
    flat-leaf parsley, leaves picked
    and chopped

80g farika (Lebanese green roasted
    wheat) or pearl barley, well rinsed

1.5 litres water

Almond and coriander topping

40g roast almonds, ground to a
    medium crumb in a mortar and
    pestle or food processor

$^1/_2$ garlic clove, crushed with
    $^1/_2$ teaspoon ground coriander
    seeds

First grind the whole aniseed, coriander seeds, cloves and caraway seeds together in a mortar and pestle or coffee grinder.

In a large saucepan, heat the olive oil over a medium heat. Season the lamb with salt and then brown it in the pan. Add the garlic and cook until slightly coloured, then add the freshly ground spices as well as the turmeric, black pepper, cinnamon and hot paprika. Cook the spices for a minute, then turn up the heat and add the celery and half the parsley. Scrape the bottom of the pan with a spoon to release any caramelised juices and spices. Cook for 5 minutes, until the celery has softened, then stir in the farika or barley and the water. Bring to the boil, skimming off any scum that appears, and season with a little more salt. Simmer for $1^1/_2$–2 hours, with a lid on, until the lamb is soft. Meanwhile, combine the almonds, garlic and ground coriander for the topping.

When the lamb is cooked, take it out and let it cool slightly before shredding the meat, discarding any bones and fatty bits. Add the meat back to the soup, along with the rest of the parsley. Taste for seasoning and serve hot, with a good amount of the almond mix sprinkled on top.

Leek and rosemary soup with Picos de Europa

The most important ingredient for making a leek soup is plenty of leeks, which makes this a perfect recipe for using up large quantities, young or old, especially during the winter months when not much else is growing on the allotment. We try not to throw away too many of the tops or outer leaves but chop them finely in a machine, unless they are tough.

Picos de Europa is the wonderful blue cheese from the Asturian mountains of the same name, but Roquefort and Stilton make good substitutes.

Serves 4

750g leeks, roots sliced off, halved lengthways and washed

6 tablespoons olive oil

80g unsalted butter

2 medium potatoes, peeled and very thinly sliced

2 garlic cloves, thinly sliced

6 grates of nutmeg

1 scant dessertspoon finely chopped fresh rosemary

1.25 litres vegetable stock, hot

2 tablespoons finely chopped fresh flat-leaf parsley

120g Picos de Europa, Roquefort or Stilton, no rind

Trim off any browned or dark green bits of the outer leaves of the leeks. Separate the light green tops and whizz them in a food processor. Slice the tender white of the leeks thinly by hand.

In a large saucepan, heat the olive oil and butter over a medium-high heat until the butter foams. Add the leeks and a good pinch of salt. Cook for 10 minutes with a lid on, stirring regularly, until softened. Turn down the heat to medium and stir in the potatoes, garlic, nutmeg and rosemary. Cook for a further 20 minutes, still stirring occasionally but now without the lid. If the leeks start to catch on the bottom of the pan, reduce the heat further and scrape up any sticking bits with a metal spoon. When the potatoes are soft and the leeks sweet, mash well with a potato masher or give them a quick whizz with a handheld blender, depending how smooth you want the soup. Add the stock, again to your desired consistency. Bring to the boil, season with salt and pepper and stir in the parsley. Serve in bowls, with the cheese crumbled on top.

Onion broth with jamón and oloroso sherry

This is a wonderfully rich and aromatic broth of sweet onion, salty jamón and nutty sherry. The sweetness of the onion is everything. Onions are full of water, which must be evaporated to concentrate the natural sugars and eliminate any hint of raw onion taste. The right size of pan is also important for the onions, which should be in a layer roughly 3cm deep as they cook. Much deeper than this and they will stew in their own juices; much shallower and they will colour before they are sweet and soft enough. We start off cooking the onions fast over a high heat, then turn the heat down to medium-low. All this may sound a little pernickety but getting the onions right makes the difference between the broth being 'okay', and 'truly memorable'.

Serves 4

5 tablespoons olive oil

1kg Spanish or mild onions, peeled
   and thinly sliced across the grain

120g jamón serrano, finely chopped

2 teaspoons fresh thyme leaves

3 grates of nutmeg

150ml medium oloroso sherry

1 litre chicken stock, preferably hot

Heat the olive oil in a large, heavy saucepan, about 25cm wide, until hot but not smoking. Add the onions with a large pinch of salt, give them a good stir and cook for 15 minutes over a high heat, stirring every 2 minutes to get them started. Now reduce the heat to medium-low and cook for 35–45 minutes, until golden brown and sweet, still stirring often so they cook evenly and do not stick to the bottom of the pan. Stir in the serrano ham, thyme and nutmeg and continue cooking for 5 minutes. Pour on the oloroso sherry and let it bubble for 2 minutes to boil off the alcohol. Add the stock, bring to a simmer and taste for seasoning. Serve with toasted rustic bread rubbed with garlic and drizzled with olive oil.

Vegetable Starters

Gözleme

We have already covered gözleme (Turkish stuffed griddle breads) in *Casa Moro* (Ebury Press, 2004), but have good reason to revisit them. A couple of years ago we went to the allotment in May, after two weeks away. There had been a lot of rain and sunshine, and as the ground had warmed up from the winter, things had gone mad. The seedlings and seeds we had planted had been completely overgrown by weeds and poppies. It looked beautiful but perhaps not what the allotment committee was hoping for. One woman, however, was delighted. When she spotted us, she came over and asked if we minded her picking the poppy leaves. Immediately curious, we nodded enthusiastically and watched as she gathered bundles of the smallest, tenderest leaves. She then beckoned us over to her plot, where we watched her roll out a flatbread and put the chopped poppy leaves and some crumbled feta on one half. She sealed the flatbread into a half-moon shape and quickly transferred it to a cast-iron dome that was resting on top of a charcoal brazier. As soon as one side was golden, it was flipped over to cook the other side, then wrapped in a napkin and handed to us. We were speechless. Not only was it utterly delicious but she had also done the weeding!

Makes 8

50g poppy leaves or rocket, mallow, dandelion or a mixture

50g sorrel

100g tender chard leaves or spinach, stalks removed

50g onion tops or spring onions

2 teaspoons olive oil

$1/2$ teaspoon ground allspice

1 quantity of Flatbread Dough (see page 80)

200g feta cheese, crumbled

60g unsalted butter, cut into 8 pieces

Wash all the leaves and the onion tops or spring onions, then dry them, leaving a little moisture on their surface (this will help them steam inside the bread). Chop them roughly and toss with the olive oil, allspice and a little salt and pepper.

When the flatbread dough has risen, divide it into 8 balls. Using a floured rolling pin, gently roll out the first ball on a generously floured surface, giving it a quarter turn each time you roll, as this keeps the shape round. The dough should be very elastic, and will start to spring back on itself

once you have got it about 5mm thick. At this point, lift it off the board and stretch it by hand, rotating as you go for an even thickness. You should be able to achieve a 25cm round of almost paper-thinness, nearly transparent at its centre.

To stuff the gözleme, place a generous handful of the leaves over one half of the dough circle, leaving a border of 1cm. Crumble the feta on top of the greens, then brush the edges of the dough with a little water to moisten slightly. Now lift the naked half of the dough over the stuffing and join the edges to make a semi-circle. Seal with your fingertips and trim off any excess dough to make a neat half-moon, leaving a border of dough no greater than 1cm. Leave on a floured surface while you make another gözleme.

Place a large frying pan over a medium heat, add a knob of the butter and when it begins to foam, gently ease the stuffed gözleme into the pan (cook 2 at a time). Fry on one side, allowing the underneath to blister and brown in places (lower the heat if it burns too quickly). Gently turn over and add another knob of butter to cook the other side. While these are cooking, you can continue to prepare another 2 gözleme and so on. We like to eat these immediately, although you can keep them warm in the oven, stacked on top of one another, while you make the rest. Serve on squares of kitchen paper to soak up any excess butter.

Dolmas

Adile is the queen of dolmas (stuffed vine leaves) on the allotment. When the young vine leaves begin to establish themselves in the spring, that is the time to take a pair of scissors to them. She collects bagfuls, and surplus leaves are blanched and frozen so homemade dolmas can be relished during winter, when there is not a leaf in sight on the vine.

Serves 4

20–25 medium-sized young vine
    leaves (fresh if possible), stalks
    pinched out
25g unsalted butter
2 tablespoons olive oil
25g pine nuts
$^1/_2$ medium onion, finely chopped
100g minced lamb
$^1/_2$ teaspoon baharat (see page 154) or
    ground allspice
30g currants
a small bunch of dill (about 10g),
    finely chopped

a few sprigs of mint (about 5g),
    finely chopped
100g short grain rice, such as
    calasparra or paella rice, soaked
    in cold water for an hour
100g cherry tomatoes, blanched,
    peeled and finely chopped
250ml water, mixed with 1
    tablespoon sugar and 2
    tablespoons lemon juice

If using fresh vine leaves, blanch them for 2 minutes in well-salted boiling water, then refresh in cold water. If using shop-bought vine leaves in brine, soak them in 2 changes of cold water to remove most of the salt.

Heat the butter in a frying pan with 1 tablespoon of the olive oil until it foams. Add the pine nuts, onion and a good pinch of salt and cook over a medium heat for about 15 minutes, until the onion is soft and sweet. Add the lamb and fry, stirring and chopping with a spoon to break it up, for about 5 minutes, until it is cooked through and any water released has evaporated (it will start to sizzle). Add the spice, currants and herbs and fry for 2 minutes more. Now stir in the drained rice and fry for a final minute. Remove from the heat, add the tomatoes, season with salt and pepper and set aside to cool.

To stuff the vine leaves, lay one flat on a board, silvery underside-up, with the tip of the leaf away from you and the stem (pinched out) pointing towards you. Lay a rounded tablespoon of the stuffing on the leaf, near the stem end, and shape with your fingers into a thin sausage (we like our dolmas long and thin). Begin to roll it away from you and, once you have made one turn, fold the ends of the 'cigar' over to seal in the stuffing. Continue to roll into a neat cylinder. Put the dolmas into a 30cm saucepan as you roll them, packing them into a single layer. It is important that they fit tightly (this helps keep them from unrolling) in a single layer, so they cook evenly.

Pour over the water–sugar–lemon solution and the remaining table-spoon of oil. If using fresh vine leaves, sprinkle over a pinch of salt (packaged ones in brine probably still have enough salt to season themselves). Cover with a circle of greaseproof paper and lay a plate on top to press the vine leaves down and stop them unrolling. Cover the pan with a tight-fitting lid, bring to the boil and simmer for 10–15 minutes. Do not allow the mixture to boil com-pletely dry, lest the sugar starts to burn. Serve hot or cold, with a squeeze of lemon and, if you like, some yoghurt.

Couscous with broad beans, cumin and yoghurt

This is one of our favourite ways of cooking the new season's broad beans, which we first encountered on the outskirts of a market in Marrakech. We were in search of soup bowls from the pottery souk and it was difficult to decide which find was the more exciting: the towers of beautiful bowls in varying shades of brown, white and green, or stumbling upon a man selling piping-hot barley couscous with broad beans and soured buttermilk, delicately flavoured with cumin.

Serves 4–6

200g couscous
1 tablespoon olive oil
350g podded broad beans, preferably
    small

1 medium bunch of coriander (about
    30g), leaves picked

Yoghurt dressing

200g good-quality Greek yoghurt,
    such as Total
$^1/_2$ garlic clove, crushed to a paste
    with a pinch of salt

2 tablespoons extra virgin olive oil
2 level teaspoons lightly pan-roasted
    cumin seeds, roughly ground
7 tablespoons (105ml) milk (or water)

For the yoghurt dressing, mix all the ingredients together in a bowl, season with a little salt and black pepper, then taste and set aside.

Put the couscous in a large bowl and wash well in cold water for a couple of minutes, changing the water twice. Drain, then add enough cold salted water to barely cover. Leave for about 5 minutes, until the couscous has completely absorbed the water. Pour over the olive oil and delicately work the couscous with the palms of your hands and your fingertips to make it light and fluffy, breaking up any lumps as you go. Fill the bottom half of a cous-coussier or steamer (the steamer should have holes small enough to prevent the couscous falling through) a third full with water and put it on a high heat to boil. Turn down the heat to a steady simmer and put on the top half. Gently lift the fluffy couscous (taking care not to compact the grains together) into the steamer, put a lid on and steam for 15–20 minutes or until hot and light. While the couscous is steaming, cook the broad beans. Blanch them in a large pan of unsalted boiling water for 4–8 minutes, until tender, then drain. Peel the skin off any that are larger than a thumbnail. Even if all the beans are small, it will look nicest if you peel half of them.

To serve, transfer the hot couscous to a mixing bowl along with two-thirds of the broad beans and two-thirds of the coriander. Pour over the yoghurt dressing, toss delicately and taste for seasoning. Serve with the remaining broad beans and coriander leaves on top.

Tortilla with onion tops

It was our allotment neighbour, Hassan, who taught us to waste nothing on the allotment. This philosophy goes for everything, not just edible produce. If you have any junk, you can be sure to find a use for it on the allotment and a skip is the best place to find some: windows to make cold frames, pallets for fences, lorry seats for chairs, old CDs on string as a bird scarer, the list is endless. Soon after we got to know Hassan, he cooked us a tortilla with onion tops. It opened our eyes to these vegetables and has changed the way we use them. Braised slowly in olive oil, the long, green leaves become sweet and succulent. Enveloped in creamy egg, they are to die for. We never throw away onion tops now and, if tortilla is not on the agenda, they find their way into a flatbread with feta or into stock. If necessary, you can use spring onions instead. Once you have mastered the technique of making a tortilla, you can be more adventurous with the ingredients: add prawns, jamón or roasted peppers.

Serves 4

9 tablespoons (135ml) olive oil, plus a little extra if necessary
750g fresh green onion tops or spring onions, cut into 3–4cm lengths

350g potatoes (Cyprus or any firm, waxy potato), peeled, cut in half lengthways, then cut into slices 2mm thick
5 or 6 large organic eggs

Place a large saucepan over a medium heat and add 4 tablespoons of the olive oil. When it is hot, add the onion tops with a pinch of salt and stir well. Braise the tops for about 10–15 minutes, stirring occasionally, until they are soft and sweet. Transfer to a colander or sieve and set aside.

Meanwhile, prepare the potatoes: season them with a generous pinch of fine sea salt and leave for 5 minutes. Heat 3 tablespoons of the oil in a 25cm frying pan over a medium-low heat and add the potatoes. Fry them very gently for about 15 minutes, until soft. You will need to stir them often, scraping any sticking bits from the bottom of the pan. The idea is that they soften without colouring (in Spain, the potatoes would be sliced thicker and simmered gently in olive oil in a deep-fat fryer). Drain off any excess oil and add the potatoes to the onions.

Crack the eggs into a mixing bowl and season with a pinch of salt and black pepper. Transfer the onions and potatoes to the bowl and mix well with the egg. If you can bear to taste raw egg, check for seasoning.

Clean the frying pan, add the remaining 2 tablespoons of oil and put it back over a high heat. When the oil begins to smoke, swirl the pan around to coat the sides with oil, then pour the egg mixture in with one hand whilst shaking the pan with the other. This helps to shape the tortilla. After 20 seconds, turn the heat to low and continue cooking for about 3–5 minutes, until the underside is set and golden. Then take a plate of similar size (too small and the tortilla will run over the edge; too big and the plate will slide off the pan as you turn) and rest it, upside down, over the pan. Using both hands and 2 cloths, carefully invert the tortilla on to the plate. This also helps shape the tortilla. The uncooked side will be fairly runny, so be careful.

Turn the heat to high again, pour a little extra olive oil into the pan if needed, then slide the tortilla back in and tuck in the edges. Cook for another 20 seconds, then turn the heat to low and continue to cook for 3–5 minutes, until the second side is golden brown. Invert on to a plate again (it will be much easier this time), and slide straight back into the pan over a low heat. Cook for another couple of minutes, then turn the tortilla a final time and cook until just firm in the middle. Remove from the heat, slide on to a plate and allow to cool slightly before eating.

Kuku – Iranian omelette with saffron

Kukus are exotic and spicy egg dishes from Iran (eggah is the Arab equivalent). We serve this with fresh, crunchy salads, such as grated raw beetroot and mint, or white cabbage and rocket. To bake the kuku, we use a 25cm cazuela or frying pan with a heat-resistant handle. We have to warn you though, that the last time we served this dish to a customer, she burst into tears! She was so disappointed that vegetable mezze was not on the menu, and totally unhappy with a plate of baked eggs and salads. It made such a strong impression on us that we haven't had this dish on the menu since. However, in the comfort and security of your own home, we think it is worth a try.

... starter, 4 as a main course

1 large aubergine, cut into 1.5cm
  cubes
50g unsalted butter
3 tablespoons olive oil
6 allspice berries, crushed (or a
  pinch of ground allspice)
1 bunch of spring onions, thinly
  sliced
6 large organic eggs
2 rounded tablespoons barberries
  or currants
2 tablespoons pine nuts or walnuts

a good pinch of saffron (about 40
  strands), soaked in 1 tablespoon
  boiling water
250g spinach, wilted in a hot frying
  pan with a little olive oil and a
  pinch of salt, then drained and
  roughly chopped
3 tablespoons finely chopped fresh
  dill
1 tablespoon finely chopped fresh
  mint

To serve

1 tablespoon barberries or currants   1 tablespoon dill sprigs

Preheat a 25cm round baking dish or ovenproof frying pan in the oven at
220°C/425°F/Gas 7.

Toss the aubergine with a good pinch of fine salt and let it stand for
5 minutes. Pat dry with kitchen paper. Heat the butter and 2 tablespoons of
the olive oil in a frying pan over a medium heat until it begins to foam. Now
add the allspice, fry for 30 seconds, then add the spring onions and a pinch of
salt. Cook for 5 minutes, stirring once or twice until soft. Add the aubergine
and continue cooking, stirring often, for 10 minutes or until tender (watch
that the onions do not burn). Remove from the heat, drain off any excess oil
and set aside.

The next bit should be done just before you want to put the omelette
in the oven. Break the eggs into a medium-sized bowl and whisk with a fork.
Season with a little salt and pepper, then stir in the aubergine mixture and
all the other ingredients except the remaining oil. Taste for seasoning.
Remove the baking dish or frying pan from the oven, swirl the last tablespoon of oil around the sides, then pour in the egg mixture. Immediately
return it to the oven and bake for 12–15 minutes, until the eggs have set and
started to brown and puff up ever so slightly. Some people, ourselves included, prefer the eggs a little runny. Leave the omelette to rest for 5 minutes
before turning out on to a plate. Serve, scattered with the extra barberries or
currants and the dill.

Coca

Think of coca as a Catalan pizza – thin, crisp and chewy, usually oblong in shape, and topped with a flavoursome concoction. In Catalunya there are as many variations on cocas as there are saints' days, and some of the best come from provincial bakeries around Barcelona. Here are our versions of two classics. We use our flatbread recipe for the dough, and olive oil instead of the more traditional coca ingredient – lard. Great for lunch, each coca will serve two as a starter or one as a main course.

Makes 4 cocas

1 quantity of Flatbread Dough (see page 80)

Spinach with pine nuts, currants and salted anchovies – enough for 2 cocas

5 tablespoons olive oil, plus an
    extra drizzle

1 large onion, finely chopped

2 tablespoons chopped fresh oregano
    or marjoram

500g spinach, washed (make sure
    the leaves are well dried –
    otherwise the cooked spinach can
    be a bit watery)

50g currants, soaked in warm water
    until plump, then drained

50g pine nuts

8 salted anchovy fillets, halved
    lengthways (optional)

Onion, red pepper and aubergine – enough for 2 cocas

1 medium aubergine, cut into
    1–1.5cm cubes

1 teaspoon fine sea salt

10 tablespoons (150ml) olive oil

$1^{1}/_{2}$ large Spanish onions, roughly
    chopped

2 red peppers, cut in half
    lengthways, seeded and thinly
    sliced

1 heaped tablespoon finely chopped
    fresh rosemary

While the flatbread dough is proving, make the toppings.

    For the spinach topping, heat the oil in a large saucepan over a medium heat. Add the chopped onion and a pinch of salt and fry, stirring occasionally, for 15 minutes or until the onion is golden and sweet. Add the oregano or marjoram and fry for a few seconds, then add the spinach a

handful at a time. Give the spinach a quick stir and cook for a few minutes, until tender. Set aside to cool and drain in a colander, then chop roughly. Stir in the currants and taste the mixture for seasoning. Set aside the pine nuts and anchovies for later.

For the onion, red pepper and aubergine topping, first toss the aubergine with the salt and set aside. Heat the olive oil in a heavy saucepan about 25cm wide and, when hot but not smoking, add the onions with a pinch of salt. Give them a good stir, and cook over a medium heat for about 15 minutes, stirring every now and then. Add the peppers and cook for 15–20 minutes, until the onions are golden and sweet and the peppers soft. Be sure to stir them often so they cook evenly and do not stick to the bottom of the pan. Blot the aubergine dry, add to the pan along with the rosemary and cook for a final 15 minutes, stirring often, until the aubergine is soft all the way through. Remove from the heat and drain off any excess oil. Check for seasoning and set aside to cool.

To make and bake the cocas, preheat the oven to its maximum setting. Divide the dough into 4 balls, and roll the first one out very thinly to make a 20 x 30cm oblong. Place it on a large baking sheet (aluminium is best) and spread half of one of the fillings evenly over the surface, right up to the edges of the dough. The spinach cocas should be topped with the pine nuts and anchovy fillets, if using, and the spinach pressed down and drizzled with a little extra oil to stop it burning. The onion, red pepper and aubergine topping is ready to go as soon as it has been spread on the dough.

Bake for 10–15 minutes, until browned and crispy underneath. While one coca is in the oven, start rolling and topping the next one. They are great served piping hot straight from the oven, or at room temperature.

Syrian fattoush

This is a beautiful variation on the famous Lebanese bread salad, with subtle sweet and sour notes. We make our own crispbread for a crisper, more delicate texture, but genuine pitta bread (not the thick and flabby supermarket version) is also good. We have a whole bed of Moroccan mint on the allotment that spreads like a weed, perfect for this salad as well as for tea.

Serves 4

1 large aubergine, cut into 1.5cm cubes and tossed with 1 teaspoon fine sea salt
8 tablespoons (120ml) olive oil
16 ripe cherry tomatoes, cut in half
4 spring onions, trimmed and finely sliced

seeds of 1 small pomegranate (about 100g)
1 small bunch of mint (about 20g), roughly chopped
1 medium bunch of flat-leaf parsley (about 40g), leaves picked

Crispbread

1 quantity of Flatbread Dough (see page 80) – or 2 pitta breads

flour for dusting
25g unsalted butter

Dressing

seeds of 1 small pomegranate (about 100g), squeezed to make juice (see Note overleaf)

$^1/_2$ small garlic clove, crushed to a paste with a pinch of salt
3 tablespoons extra virgin olive oil

Preheat the oven to 180°C/350°F/Gas 4.

First make the crispbread. Take a quarter of the flatbread dough (use the remainder for another recipe, or shape it into loaves – less than one quantity of flatbread dough is difficult to knead as it is such a small amount) and divide it into 2 rounds. Roll out and stretch each one until it is extremely thin and almost translucent, about 25cm in diameter. Lightly dust with flour. Put a large frying pan over a medium–high heat and, when hot, place one of the flatbreads in it. Cook until lightly coloured underneath, then invert to cook the other side. Remove and leave to cool. Meanwhile, do the same for the second flatbread. If using shop-bought pitta, just carefully split them in half lengthways.

Melt the butter and brush it on both sides of the bread. Place the breads on a rack in the middle of the oven and bake until golden – about 5–10 minutes for paper-thin homemade flatbread, 10–15 minutes for thicker pitta bread. Remove from the oven and leave to cool.

For the dressing, mix all the ingredients together and season with salt and pepper to taste.

For the aubergine, rinse off the salt and dry well with kitchen paper. Heat up the olive oil in a large frying pan or wok over a high heat and fry the aubergine for about 10 minutes, until soft and deep golden brown. Drain on kitchen paper and keep warm.

To serve the salad, combine two-thirds of the crispbread with the tomatoes, spring onions, aubergine, two-thirds of the pomegranate seeds and the herbs in a large salad bowl, breaking up the bread with your hands as you go. Now pour on the dressing and toss very gently. Taste for seasoning and serve with the remaining crispbread and pomegranate seeds on top.

Note

To make pomegranate juice, cut the pomegranate in half, break open each half and pick out the seeds, being careful not to include any of the pith, as it is very bitter. Put the seeds in a sieve set over a bowl and crush them with your hands as much as possible to extract the juice. Then push them against the sieve with the back of a large spoon to extract as much remaining juice as you can.

Sweetcorn with cumin butter

Grilling vegetables directly over charcoal or baking them in the embers is both satisfying and delicious. Sweetcorn benefits greatly from being cooked as soon as it is picked, as some varieties can turn starchy over time. There is nowhere easier to do this than on the allotment, as it takes only about 30 seconds from plant to barbecue. We leave a layer of leaves on the sweetcorn so they act like an inbuilt covering of foil, protecting the kernels within. Potatoes, sweet potatoes and beetroot wrapped in foil and put in the embers are also fantastic. Cumin is a miracle of a spice with its ability to transform ingredients single-handedly. We use it more than any other spice, as it is used in all the countries we cover at Moro.

Serves 4

4 sweetcorn, in their husks, stalks on
75g unsalted butter, preferably
    caramelised (see page 6)

1 teaspoon freshly ground cumin
    mixed with 1 teaspoon Maldon
    sea salt

Pull most of the husks off the corn, leaving a double layer of leaves to protect the kernels. Snapping the extra leaves off at the base should, if you're lucky, leave you a couple of centimetres of stalk to hold and turn the corn by as it cooks. Place the sweetcorn over a fairly low barbecue. Grill, turning often, for about 20 minutes, until the leaves are partly charred. To eat, just peel off the leaves and fibres, spoon over the butter and sprinkle with the cumin salt.

Artichokes braised with mushrooms

Artichokes and cardoons tend to be grown around the perimeter of vegetable plots, presumably because they are so tall, creating a natural barrier – as we have seen in Hackney and in Spain. One neighbour, Ali, noticed me planting some artichoke plants and said, 'You can't do it like that.' (I think they were too close together.) Anyway, after two years they had flourished and produced as many as 16 artichokes on one plant. Ali then asked us whether we would mind him taking a cutting from that plant when we split it during the winter. It made me smile, as I would never have imagined him asking that. He is a much better gardener than I.

Serves 4

4 very large or 8 medium globe
    artichokes
$^1/_2$ lemon
6 tablespoons olive oil
2 garlic cloves, finely chopped
$^1/_2$ teaspoon fennel seeds
4 tablespoons finely chopped fresh
    flat-leaf parsley

250g oyster mushrooms, any long
    stems removed
100ml fino sherry (or white wine)
50ml water
4 thick slices of rustic bread,
    toasted, gently rubbed with garlic
    and drizzled with olive oil

To prepare the artichokes, have ready a bowl of cold water with the lemon juice squeezed in and the squeezed lemon half bobbing around in it. Work on one artichoke at a time, and get it in the lemony water quickly to stop it going brown, before starting on the next one. The general rule when preparing artichokes is that what is green is tough and what is yellow is tender. Cut off the stalk from the base, peel about 2mm off all around the stalk, cut it into 2cm lengths and put it in the water. Now carefully snap or pull off the layers of tough, green outer leaves until you reach the ones that are mostly yellow, and therefore tender. Cut the darker tips off these, then peel the tough green outside of the base (heart) of the artichoke with a small sharp knife until you see yellow. Scrape out all the furry choke from inside the artichoke with a teaspoon. Cut the prepared artichoke in half lengthways and then cut each half into small wedges no more than 1–1.5cm wide. Place in the water and start on the next one. Prepare all the artichokes in this way.

    Just before cooking the artichokes, drain them well and toss with a generous pinch of salt. Heat the oil in a wide saucepan over a medium heat, add the artichokes and fry for 15 minutes, stirring often, until golden and nearly tender. Add the garlic, fennel seeds and half the parsley, fry for a moment until the garlic begins to colour, then add the oyster mushrooms, placing them in between the artichokes. Put a lid on the pan and cook for a further 5–8 minutes, removing the lid every minute or so to stir and check on the dish (you must watch that the garlic doesn't burn). When the mushrooms are tender, and hopefully partly caramelised, remove the lid and add the sherry. Let it bubble for a minute or two, until very little juice remains, then remove from the heat and stir in the water and the remaining parsley. Taste for seasoning before spooning the mixture over the warm toast.

Three tahini dips: avocado, beetroot and pumpkin

We all know the classic Lebanese tahini dips, baba ghanoush (aubergine and tahini) and hummus (chickpea and tahini). Here are some variations on the theme. To scoop up the dips, use warm Flatbread (page 80), Crispbread (page 50), pitta and crudités.

Serves 4

Avocado

2 or 3 ripe avocados (about 500g in total), stoned and peeled

2 tablespoons lemon juice

2 tablespoons tahini

3 tablespoons extra virgin olive oil, plus an extra drizzle

1 garlic clove, crushed to a smooth paste with a pinch of salt

2 tablespoons finely chopped fresh mint

a pinch of dried Turkish (mild) chilli flakes (optional)

Place the avocado flesh, lemon juice, tahini, oil and garlic in a food processor and whizz until smooth. Transfer to a mixing bowl, add the mint and season to taste with salt and pepper. Serve with an extra drizzle of olive oil, and if you like, a scattering of chilli flakes.

Beetroot

600g raw beetroot, trimmed of stalks and washed well (leave the skin on)

1 garlic clove, crushed to a paste with a pinch of salt

6 tablespoons extra virgin olive oil

2 tablespoons tahini

2 tablespoons finely chopped fresh mint

2 dessertspoons red wine vinegar

Place the beetroot in a saucepan, fill with salted cold water and cover with a lid. Bring to the boil over a high heat, then turn down the heat to medium and simmer until the beetroot are completely tender in the middle. This will take $1^1/_2$–2 hours, depending on their size. They are done when you can slip a sharp knife easily into the centre, rather like testing to see if a potato is cooked. Remove from the heat, drain in a colander and, under cold running water, slide off the skin. Transfer the beetroot to a food processor with the

garlic, oil and tahini and whizz until smooth. Transfer to a mixing bowl and add the mint and vinegar. Season with salt and pepper to taste.

Pumpkin

1kg pumpkin or squash, peeled and seeded (about 600g prepared flesh), then cut into 3cm chunks

6 tablespoons extra virgin olive oil

$1/4$ heaped teaspoon freshly ground cinnamon

$1/2$ small garlic clove, crushed with a pinch of salt

2 tablespoons tahini

1 tablespoon lemon juice

2 tablespoons pine nuts, lightly toasted

Preheat the oven to 220°C/425°F/Gas 7.

Place the pumpkin in a roasting tray and drizzle over 2 tablespoons of the olive oil. Sprinkle with the cinnamon and a good pinch of salt and black pepper and toss well. Cover tightly with aluminium foil and roast for 40 minutes, until very soft. Uncover and return to the oven for 10 minutes, to dry out any excess moisture. Transfer the pumpkin to a food processor and add the garlic, tahini, lemon juice and the remaining olive oil. Purée until smooth and then check for seasoning. Spread the purée out on a plate and sprinkle with the pine nuts.

Spiced labneh with beetroot and fennel

Raw beetroot is often overlooked as an ingredient. But stop right here and give it a try. If you can, try to find, or grow, the stripy Chioggia variety as well as normal ones. They have an extraordinary psychedelic Sixties look about them, which fades the second they are cooked. Isn't nature wonderful? Use the beetroot tops as you would spinach in another dish.

If you don't want to make your own labneh, you could use 200g good-quality Greek yoghurt, such as Total, mixed with 100g cream cheese.

Serves 4

1 small garlic clove, crushed to a
    paste with a pinch of salt
1 large green chilli, finely chopped
1½ teaspoons fenugreek seeds,
    soaked for 2 hours in 3 changes
    of freshly boiled water
1 dessertspoon black onion seeds
250g small raw beetroot
1 large, leafy fennel bulb (about
    400g), outer layer removed,
    young leaves kept aside

1 tablespoon lemon juice
½ tablespoon red wine vinegar
3 tablespoons extra virgin olive oil,
    plus an extra drizzle
Flatbreads (see page 80) or a loaf of
    Turkish bread, to serve

Homemade labneh

400g good-quality Greek yoghurt,
    such as Total

¼–½ teaspoon fine sea salt, to taste

To make the labneh, place the yoghurt in a mixing bowl and stir in the salt so
you can just taste it. Line another bowl with a piece of muslin or other fine
cloth and spoon the yoghurt into the centre. Draw up the corners of the cloth
and secure with string or an elastic band. Suspend over a sink or bowl and
leave overnight for the whey to drain out.

The next day, unwrap the labneh and put it in a bowl. Stir the garlic,
chilli, fenugreek and half the black onion seeds through the labneh and season
with salt if needed. Slice the beetroot and fennel as thinly as possible and toss
them with the lemon juice, vinegar and oil. Season with salt and pepper.

To serve, spread the labneh on one half of a plate, sprinkle with the
remaining black onion seeds and drizzle with olive oil. Put the beetroot salad
on the other side, topped with the reserved young fennel leaves. Serve accompanied with the flatbreads or Turkish bread.

Setas a la plancha

Oyster mushrooms seem to grow consistently well all year. We have started trying to grow them just for fun, as we got a mushroom log for Christmas and many seed catalogues sell the spores. We have stared at the log for three months now and it has done nothing. Still, maybe spring will activate the spores, or maybe we are just staring at the wrong log! What will make the difference to the quality of this salad, though, is good-quality Spanish vinegar, oil and fresh garlic (not stale). At Moro in the late summer we make this salad using half oyster mushrooms and half Scottish girolles. Oyster mushrooms can be eaten raw, so the point of searing them on one side is to soften them slightly but mostly to give a complexity of flavour. Enjoy this salad warm or at room temperature, either on its own or with chicken or pork.

Serves 4

500g oyster mushrooms, or a
    mixture of half oyster, half
    girolles
4 tablespoons extra virgin olive oil
1–2 teaspoons posh vinegar (sherry,
    or a good red wine vinegar such
    as Forum)

1 garlic clove, very finely chopped
    at the last minute
1 tablespoon roughly chopped fresh
    flat-leaf parsley
1 tablespoon finely chopped fresh
    oregano

Trim excessive stalks from the mushrooms. Toss the mushrooms with salt and pepper and 3 tablespoons of the oil. Heat a very wide (30cm) frying pan over a high heat. When good and hot, place a layer of mushrooms in the pan, gill-side down. Gently press down on the mushrooms. When they are nicely browned, transfer to a bowl and place another layer of mushrooms in the pan. Repeat until you have finished all your mushrooms. Toss all the cooked mushrooms with the remaining tablespoon of oil, plus the vinegar, garlic and herbs, and season with salt and pepper. We like to eat this with good crusty bread.

Porcini and barley salad with sweet herbs

At Moro, we use fresh porcini mushrooms for this dish. This is the mushroom probably closest to our hearts, not only because of its unsurpassably delicate sweetness and texture but because when I was a little girl I used to forage for them in the south of France near my Grandma's. The taste brings back many happy memories.

If you can't get hold of farika (the Lebanese green roasted wheat), then double the quantity of pearl barley in this recipe.

Serves 4

75g farika

75g pearl barley

4 tablespoons olive oil

300g young, firm porcini (or field mushrooms), cut across into even 4–5mm slices

a small bunch of parsley (about 20g), leaves picked

a small bunch of tarragon (about 15g), leaves picked

a small bunch of dill (about 15g), leaves picked

2 tablespoons very finely chopped red onion

Dressing

1–2 dessertspoons lemon juice, to taste

3 tablespoons extra virgin olive oil

2 tablespoons water

Boil the farika for 10–15 minutes, until 'al dente', then drain, season with salt and pepper and set aside to cool. In a separate pan, boil the pearl barley for about 20–30 minutes or until just tender, then drain, season and leave to cool.

Heat 2 tablespoons of the oil in a large frying pan over a high heat. Season the mushrooms with a little salt and pepper and fry in batches, one layer at a time, turning once, until coloured and just soft; they should take about 15–20 seconds per side. Add extra oil as necessary between batches until they are all done. Allow the mushrooms to cool slightly, then toss with the farika, barley, herbs and onion. Make a dressing by whisking together the lemon juice, olive oil, water and some salt and pepper and dress the salad. Check for seasoning and serve immediately.

Bitter leaves with tahini and crispy caramelised onions

If you're a fan of bitter flavours, then this is the one for you. Combined with the lemony tahini and sweet onion, the bitter leaves are very good indeed. You can eat this on its own, but it is also excellent accompanying fish or lamb. Winter leaves, such as chicory, dandelion, radicchio and trevise, are best for this dish but you could use just white chicory. Samuel is quite rightly proud of his winter leaves: green chicory, mâche and dandelion are all abundant.

Serves 4

40g unsalted butter

2 tablespoons olive oil

2 heads of white or green chicory, cut in half lengthways

1 head of trevise or small Cos lettuce, cut in quarters lengthways

1 head of radicchio, cut into quarters (or 2 heads if you can't get trevise or Cos)

100g frisée salad or dandelion

1 quantity of Tahini Sauce (see page 265)

2 tablespoons roughly chopped fresh flat-leaf parsley

a squeeze of lemon

Crispy caramelised onions

1 very large Spanish onion

vegetable oil for frying

First prepare the onions. Careful slicing is crucial for beautifully crispy, evenly caramelised onions, so first halve and peel the onion, then slice it across the grain as consistently thinly as possible. If you have a mandolin, now may be the time to use it. Heat 8–10mm depth of vegetable oil in a wide saucepan over a high heat. When it is hot but not smoking, add a 1cm layer of the shaved onions and reduce the heat to medium. Fry, stirring often, until they are an even golden colour (they will get a little darker after you take them out of the pan). Drain and spread out on kitchen paper to cool, then repeat the process (you may need to top up the oil) until you have used all the onions – you can cook this quantity in 2 batches in a 30cm pan. The onions can be cooked ahead of time.

To cook the leaves, place a large (30cm) frying pan over a medium heat and add the butter and olive oil. When the butter begins to foam, add the chicory, trevise and radicchio, season with a little salt and pepper and fry for about 10 minutes, until caramelised and light brown on one side. Turn over and repeat for the other side. As you turn the chicory over, add the frisée or dandelion to the gaps in the pan, season and push gently until wilted. When the chicory and other leaves are lightly browned all over, remove from the heat and transfer to a warm plate. Drizzle over the tahini sauce, sprinkle with the crispy caramelised onions and chopped parsley and finish with a squeeze of lemon.

Fish Starters

Grilled asparagus with bottarga

A few years ago we bought some asparagus crowns to plant in the allotment. Growing asparagus is an investment, mainly of time, as you have to wait at least two years before the plants bear any usable crop. And before you start, you must make a special asparagus bed, which involves digging rather a lot of sand into the earth. But it was worth it, and we relished our first asparagus for a year or so, until disaster struck. Short of time and needing to get the allotment soil ready for planting, one of our kitchen porters volunteered to help dig over the earth for us with a Rotavator. But we were not clear enough which beds needed digging and arrived to find that our asparagus plants and precious wild bluebells, which had been growing happily around the edge of the beds, had been churned to a pulp!

Bottarga (which comes from the Arabic word meaning 'to cure'), or cured mullet roe, is delicious grated over asparagus. We grill the asparagus spears after they have been blanched, although this is not essential.

Serves 4

1kg firm green asparagus	juice of $^1/_2$ lemon
4 tablespoons extra virgin olive oil	100g bottarga (cured mullet roe), grated on a fine grater

Preheat a griddle to smoking-hot, or light a barbecue 30 minutes before you start.

The root end of asparagus can be woody and stringy. Gently flex the very end of each spear until the stem snaps off at its natural break, or peel the ends. Rinse and drain the spears.

When you are ready to cook the asparagus, bring a wide saucepan of well-salted water to the boil. Put the asparagus in and bring back to the boil with the lid on, then remove the lid. Boil for 2–3 minutes, depending on thickness, until the asparagus is almost tender – or for a minute longer, until tender, if you are not planning to grill it. Drain the asparagus carefully, and put them on the griddle or barbecue. When the asparagus are lightly charred on one side, roll them over and char the other side. Remove and place in a bowl. Pour over the olive oil and lemon juice, season with salt and pepper and place on a plate. Sprinkle with the bottarga and serve immediately.

Salt cod carpaccio with broad beans

The great thing about growing your own broad beans, and indeed any vegetable, is that you decide when they are ready to pick, and are not dependent on the whim of a commercial grower.

The wonderful Hispanophile and writer, Michael Jacobs, telephoned last April when the new broad beans were in season in Spain to tell us what he had just been eating at a gastronomic society in the province of Jaén. We loved the beauty and simplicity of the dish, and the next day it was on the menu. It is best made with the more expensive, thick salt cod loin, which is less cured, softer and therefore easier to slice. The length of time you soak the salt cod depends on its saltiness; taste a little piece to check if it is palatable.

Serves 4

200g podded young broad beans, no larger than a thumbnail

200g salt cod, soaked for 24–36 hours in 3 or 4 changes of abundant cold water

20–30 tiny mint leaves, or shredded mint leaves if larger

grated zest of $^1/_2$ lemon

4 tablespoons extra virgin olive oil

2 teaspoons (a good squeeze) lemon juice

Blanch the broad beans for 2–4 minutes in unsalted boiling water. Drain and refresh in cold water, then peel off the outer skin, leaving the smallest ones with the skin on.

Drain the salt cod, place it skin-down on a board and use tweezers or fine pliers to remove any small bones. To slice, use a razor-sharp non-serrated knife, keep the blade wet, and support the flesh of the fish with the palm of your hand as you cut wafer-thin slices from it. Don't worry if the slices tear – thinner and slightly ragged is better than unbroken but thick. Arrange the slices flat, in a single layer, on 4 cool plates. Scatter with the broad beans, mint and lemon zest. Stir together the oil and lemon juice to make a dressing, season with black pepper and spoon it over the fish. You will probably not need to add any salt.

Salmorejo with prawns, tomato and avocado

We first had this light and unusual starter at **Mesón Redonda** in Jerez. We jokingly refer to it as the 'prawn cocktail of Andalucía', yet it is something much more refined. Salmorejo is usually served as a soup but it can also be a sauce.

Serves 4

2 ripe avocados

1 quantity of chilled Salmorejo
   Sauce (see page 262), made with
   sherry vinegar rather than red
   wine vinegar

8 cherry tomatoes, cut in half

$^1/_2$ new season's onion (or $^1/_2$ small
   red onion), very thinly sliced

300g shell-on cooked North Atlantic
   prawns, peeled

1 heaped tablespoon fresh oregano,
   chopped if the leaves are large

Cut each avocado in half lengthways, take out the stone and remove the skin. Cut each half lengthways into slices 5mm thick, leaving them joined together at the narrow end. Very gently spread out each half into a subtle fan shape. Check the salmorejo for seasoning, spoon it on to a large plate right up to the inner rim, then tactically place the 4 fanned-out avocado halves on it and, in between them, the tomato halves. Scatter the onion, prawns and oregano all over and serve immediately. Bizarre but quite yummy.

Squid, celery and preserved lemon salad

We are always thrilled to be the champions of unglamorous vegetables. Celery is one vegetable that many find unexciting, but it grows very well in the UK and has a delightful, aromatic flavour. When it is lightly cooked and mixed with preserved lemon, all its best qualities shine through. Without the squid, this salad accompanies fish and chicken very successfully.

Serves 4

800g whole medium squid (or 600g cleaned squid)

6 tablespoons olive oil

20g preserved lemon rind (about $1/2$ preserved lemon, or citron confit, pulp removed), rinsed and finely chopped

$1/2$ teaspoon whole cumin seeds

2 garlic cloves, thinly sliced

1 large head of celery, cut into slices 7–10mm thick

100ml water

1 small bunch of coriander (about 20g), leaves picked and roughly chopped

12 green olives (optional)

To serve (optional)

2 bunches of wild rocket

a squeeze of lemon

3 tablespoons extra virgin olive oil

If using whole squid, you will need to clean them: gently pull off the wings and set them aside, then pull off the head, taking as much of the guts out of the body sac with it as possible. Slice off the tentacles in front of the eyes and remove the beak. Cut the tentacles into bunches of 2 or 3. Make a slit down the length of the body sac to open it flat, then remove the transparent quill and any more guts from the inside. Wash the body under a running tap and remove any pink membrane. Slice the body in strips, about 1.5 x 5cm. Wash the wings, again removing any pink membrane, and cut them into 1cm strips.

Heat 4 tablespoons of the olive oil in a wide frying pan over a medium heat and add the preserved lemon, cumin and garlic. Fry until they just begin to colour, then add the celery. Cook, stirring often, for 5–10 minutes – it will turn a vivid green. Add the water and cook for another 5 minutes, until it has reduced by two-thirds and the celery is tender, yet still has a little crunch.

Transfer the celery to a bowl, taking care to scrape every bit from the pan. Return the pan to a high heat until smoking, then add the remaining oil and the squid. Do not stir for the first minute, so the squid gets some colour from the bottom of the pan, then season with a little salt and pepper and stir occasionally until it loses all translucency and is just tender. Turn off the heat, return the celery to the pan, add the coriander and olives and toss in with the squid. Check for seasoning.

Serve immediately as a warm salad, or chill if you prefer. If serving with the rocket topping, toss the rocket with the lemon and extra virgin olive oil before arranging on 4 plates and spooning the celery and squid on top.

Labneh with anchovies, red chilli and cucumber

As a boy in my lunch breaks at school, I would be free to wander the streets of London looking for the best way to spend a pound on lunch. My favourite haunt was Wilma's Sandwich Bar. After months of eating cheese and tomato sandwiches, I heard a man in the queue asking for a cream cheese, black pepper and anchovy sandwich. Not knowing quite what to expect, but ever the adventurer, I asked for 'one of the same, please'. The blissful taste still represents the best sort of food we do at Moro: three simple flavours jostling in the mouth to create something exciting. This starter was an attempt to recapture that moment. At Moro, we make our own flatbread (see below), or use good quality pitta bread.

Serves 4

1 quantity of homemade Labneh (strained yoghurt cheese – see page 61), or use 200g good-quality Greek yoghurt, such as Total, mixed with 100g cream cheese and seasoned with a little salt

8 salted anchovy fillets, cut in half lengthways

1 fresh, large, mildish red chilli, cut in half lengthways, seeded and thinly sliced

1 tablespoon finely shredded fresh mint

$1/2$ teaspoon black onion seeds

2 tablespoons olive oil

1 large cucumber, peeled, cut in half across and then each half into long thin wedges

Flatbread dough

225g unbleached strong white bread flour, plus extra for dusting

$3/4$ teaspoon fine sea salt

$1/2$ teaspoon dried yeast

150ml tepid water

1 tablespoon olive oil

To make the flatbread dough, place the flour and salt in a large mixing bowl. Dissolve the yeast in the water and add the oil. Now make a well in the middle of the flour and pour in the yeast mixture a little at a time, mixing constantly. We like to do this by hand, squelching out the lumps as they appear. When all the yeast mixture has been incorporated, transfer the dough to a floured surface and knead well for at least 5 minutes. If the dough is still sticky, add a little more flour; if it is stiff, a little more water. It is ready when no longer tacky but soft, elastic and smooth. Put the dough back in the bowl, cover with a cloth and leave to rise in a warm place until doubled in bulk – approximately 1–2 hours.

Preheat the oven to 230°C/450°F/Gas 8. Divide the dough into 8 balls. On a very well-floured surface, roll out each piece into a rough circle 3mm thick. Transfer them to 2 large, lightly floured baking sheets and put them in the hot oven immediately. Bake for 5–10 minutes, until each bread has partially bubbled up and coloured slightly, yet is not totally crisp.

Spread the labneh flat on a plate with the back of a spoon. Arrange the anchovy fillets in criss-cross fashion over the top and scatter with the chilli, mint and onion seeds. Drizzle with the olive oil. Serve with the cucumber and warm flatbreads on the side.

Tuna with judion beans, fennel and sherry vinegar

Both Florence fennel and herb fennel are wonderfully optimistic plants to have in any garden or allotment. They grow all the way through the winter and are sculptural as well as delicate, only looking slightly down in the dumps after being sat on by snow. You can often find flowers (or pollen) and seeds on the same plant at the same time. The seeds have a wonderful fresh aniseed flavour, perfect for this salad. Judion beans are large, plump Spanish butter beans.

Serves 4

150g dried judion beans or best-quality butter beans, soaked in cold water overnight (you could use 300g bottled or tinned butter beans instead)

2 large red peppers (the long, sweet romanos are best)

1 large fennel bulb, trimmed, cut in half and thinly sliced (reserve any young leaves)

$^1/_2$ smallish red onion, thinly sliced

1 small bunch (about 20g) of young fennel tops (or flat-leaf parsley)

1 heaped tablespoon fresh oregano leaves

2 fresh tuna steaks, each about 200g, cut in half

4 tablespoons extra virgin olive oil

1 teaspoon fresh or dry fennel seeds (or flowers), lightly crushed

a squeeze of lemon

2 teaspoons sherry vinegar or sweet red wine vinegar, such as Forum (if you don't have any, use good-quality red wine vinegar with a pinch of sugar)

If using soaked dried butter beans, drain them, rinse in a colander, then place in a large pan and cover generously with cold water. Bring to the boil and simmer gently for 1–2 hours, until tender. Pour off the cooking liquor until it is level with the beans, season with salt and pepper, then set aside and keep warm. If using bottled or tinned beans, wash off the liquid and place them in a small saucepan with a little water. Warm through and set aside.

Preheat a griddle pan or barbecue and grill the peppers until they are charred and softened. Peel and seed them, then tear them into strips. Put the sliced fennel, red onion, strips of red pepper, fennel tops, chopped if very long, and oregano into a mixing bowl.

Season the tuna with salt, brush it with 1 tablespoon of the olive oil and sprinkle with the fennel seeds. Just before you cook the tuna (which takes a matter of seconds), drain the warm butter beans and add them to your mixing bowl. Drizzle with the remaining olive oil, plus the lemon and vinegar, season and toss carefully. Sear the tuna on the griddle or barbecue for a maximum of 30 seconds on one side, then flip over to cook the other side. We like our tuna medium rare to rare in the middle. Lay the salad on a dish with the tuna on top and sprinkle with the fennel leaves. Eat immediately.

Mackerel escabeche

This ancient way of preserving heightens the delicate, silky texture of the mackerel. We serve this with a fennel, radish and orange salad. When blood oranges are in season, you can use a mixture of navel and blood oranges.

Serves 4

2 tablespoons olive oil
1 small red onion, thinly sliced

2 small-medium or 1 very large
   mackerel, filleted and pin-boned

Escabeche marinade

6 tablespoons sherry vinegar
6 tablespoons sweet red wine
   vinegar, Forum balsamic
1 dried (guindilla) chilli pepper,
   seeded and thinly sliced
2 teaspoons coriander seeds

1 teaspoon black peppercorns
a few parsley stalks (optional)
1 teaspoon sugar
4 fresh bay leaves
2 teaspoons fine sea salt
250ml water

Salad

1 teaspoon lemon juice
3 tablespoons extra virgin olive oil
10 radishes, topped, tailed and sliced
1 fennel bulb, trimmed and thinly
   sliced (reserve the leaves)

2 medium oranges, peeled with a
   knife, removing all pith, then
   sliced into thin rounds
1 small bunch of flat-leaf parsley,
   leaves picked and chopped

In a saucepan, bring all the marinade ingredients to the boil, then remove from the heat and leave to steep for 5–10 minutes. Meanwhile, heat the oil in a large frying pan over a high heat. Season the mackerel fillets and add to the pan to seal, flesh-side only, for 30 seconds. Lay the fillets, skin-side up, in a snug-fitting dish and sprinkle with the onion. Pour over the hot marinade to cover, then leave to cool. Cover the dish with cling film and put in the fridge for a few hours or overnight. Half an hour before you are ready to eat, take the mackerel out of the fridge. For the salad, squeeze the lemon juice into a bowl, season with salt and pepper and stir in the oil. Toss the rest of the salad ingredients with the dressing. Allow to stand for a couple of minutes, then toss again. Scatter with the fennel leaves. Divide the salad between 4 plates, break the mackerel into large flakes and lay them on top.

Grilled sardines with fennel, garlic and chilli

It is a joy each year to see where the self-seeded fennel will pop up. Growing fennel as a herb is a doddle, yet with Florentine fennel, achieving a plump base for frying and salads is a bit more problematic.

You can use mackerel instead of sardines here, if you prefer.

Serves 4

8 fresh sardines (or 4 portion-sized mackerel fillets)

To serve

1 large fennel bulb (and leaves), trimmed and finely chopped

1 small bunch (about 20g) of young fennel tops, or flat-leaf parsley, chopped

2 small garlic cloves, finely chopped

2 long, fresh green chillies, seeded and finely chopped

1 lemon in halves or quarters

If you are grilling over charcoal, light it 20–30 minutes before you wish to cook. If you are grilling under a domestic grill, turn it to a high heat 5 minutes before you are ready. Or heat a ridged griddle pan until really hot.

Scaling sardines is easy: just hold each fish under running water and rub from tail to head, as you would a bar of soap. Most of the scales will fall away and any left behind will be easily visible. To gut the fish, make a slit up the length of the belly with a sharp knife or scissors. Wash out the interior of the belly under running water and cut off the fins with scissors (a fishmonger could easily do all of this in a couple of minutes). Pat the sardines dry with kitchen paper. In a large bowl, toss the sardines with a generous pinch of sea salt, cover and chill for about half an hour.

Grill the sardines for about 2–3 minutes on either side. The skin should be slightly charred and the flesh cooked through to the bone but still juicy. Lay them on a large plate and sprinkle the chopped fennel, fennel tops or parsley, garlic and chilli all over. Serve with the lemon.

Clams with artichokes

We ate a variation on this recipe, made with cardoons rather than artichokes, at the restaurant in Bilbao's Guggenheim Museum. Whilst cardoons are common in Spain (as I write this, I am watching my neighbour in the field opposite our house in Spain cut down a huge bundle of cardoon leaves), in the UK artichokes are much more popular, so we have used them instead. But now, a revelation! Young artichoke leaves taste just as good as cardoons! So when an established artichoke plant needs thinning, instead of taking a cutting, we simply eat the stalks. To prepare them, trim off and discard the leafy part so the stalks look like a large stick of celery, then peel the outside of the stalk well with a potato peeler to remove any stringy bits. Cut into slices 1–2cm thick and boil in salted water for 15–20 minutes, until they are quite soft and the bitter taste has been replaced by a mild artichoke flavour.

Serves 4

3 large globe artichokes (and/or
    prepared and boiled leaves – see
    above)
600g small clams, such as venus or
    palourdes (or mussels)
6 tablespoons olive oil
2 garlic cloves, finely chopped

1 teaspoon fennel seeds
2 teaspoons plain flour
100ml manzanilla or fino sherry (or
    white wine)
5 tablespoons finely chopped
    fresh flat-leaf parsley

To prepare the artichokes, see page 55. Cut them into 1cm segments and cook immediately, or store in a bowl of water with a good squeeze of lemon for up to an hour or two to prevent them discolouring.

Wash the clams under cold water and rinse thoroughly, discarding any open ones that don't close when tapped on the worktop. Heat the oil in a large saucepan over a medium heat. Add the artichoke hearts and/or stalks, season with salt and pepper and fry gently for about 10 minutes, stirring occasionally, until golden brown and almost tender. Now add the garlic and fennel seeds and fry for a few seconds, until the garlic just begins to colour. Sprinkle in the flour, then add the clams, turn up the heat and toss the clams around with the garlic and oil. Pour in the sherry and add half the parsley, shaking the pan as you go. Cover and cook over a high heat for about 2 minutes, until the clams begin to open. Remove the lid and continue to cook for a minute or two more, until they have all opened (discard any stubborn ones that remain closed). Taste for seasoning; the clams may not need any salt. Sprinkle over the rest of the parsley and serve with bread, plus spoons for drinking the sauce.

Clams with fino sherry and jamón

As with all our clam recipes, mussels can be substituted. The addition of crisp, golden pieces of bread scattered on top to finish the dish is pleasing both visually and texturally.

Serves 4

150g rustic white bread, such as
    sourdough or ciabatta (day-old
    bread is best), crusts removed
7 tablespoons (105ml) olive oil
1kg small clams, such as palourdes
    or venus (or use mussels)
2 garlic cloves, finely chopped

$^1/_2$ teaspoon fennel seeds
30g jamón serrano or ibérico, cut
    into short matchsticks
4 tablespoons finely chopped fresh
    flat-leaf parsley
150ml fino or manzanilla sherry
a drizzle of extra virgin olive oil

Preheat the oven to 190°C/375°F/Gas 5.

First make the croûtons. Tear the bread into little pieces, about 1cm square, toss well with 3 tablespoons of the olive oil, then spread on a baking tray and bake for 15–20 minutes until crisp and golden.

Wash the clams under cold water, then rinse thoroughly, discarding any open ones that don't close when tapped on a worktop. Place a large frying pan over a medium-high heat and add the remaining olive oil. When hot, add the garlic, fennel seeds, jamón and half the parsley and fry for 30 seconds, until the garlic begins to colour. Then add the clams, stir for a moment, and add the sherry. Let it bubble for 30 seconds, put the lid on the pan and cook for 2–3 minutes, shaking the pan occasionally, until most of the clams have opened. Remove the lid, scatter with the croûtons and remaining parsley and cook for a minute more, until all the clams have opened (discard any that refuse to do so). Drizzle a little of your best olive oil on top and serve immediately.

Brandada

This salt cod purée can also be made with undyed smoked haddock, which does not need to be soaked. For a flashier finish, we spoon a little inexpensive avruga caviar on top, and chives – a wonderful allotment herb, which, if you do not cut it too often, produces pretty purple flowers. One of the first things we planted in the allotment was a bay tree, as the fresh, spicy leaves really make a difference, especially to this dish. This tree and the huge one in our garden provide Moro with an unlimited supply.

Serves 4

500ml milk

$^1/_4$ medium onion, peeled

5 black peppercorns

1 garlic clove, peeled

2 fresh bay leaves

110g salt cod, soaked in cold water in the fridge for 18–24 hours, changing the water 2 or 3 times

1 medium potato (about 200g), peeled and cut into slices 1cm thick

4 tablespoons extra virgin olive oil, plus an extra drizzle

To serve

50g avruga caviar (optional)

2 level tablespoons finely chopped fresh chives

2 tinned piquillo peppers (or 1 large red pepper, grilled or roasted, peeled and seeded), torn into strips (optional)

$^1/_2$ small red onion, sliced thinly

2 tablespoons whole parsley leaves dressed with olive oil and lemon

1 handful of caperberries or capers

Place a saucepan over a medium–high heat and add the milk, onion, pepper-corns, garlic clove and bay. Bring to a simmer, then add the salt cod and simmer gently for 2–4 minutes, until the salt cod is just cooked and the fish flakes easily (salt cod will stay more juicy and tender if cooked gently). With a slotted spoon, carefully lift out the salt cod and set aside to cool on a large plate. Now add the potato to the same saucepan of simmering milk and boil gently until soft. When the salt cod is just cool enough to handle (but still quite warm, as it becomes stubborn and gluey when cold), go through the flesh, discarding any skin or bones. Shred the cod finely between your fingers, feeling for small bones as you go, until there are no hard bits, just soft fibre.

When the potato is cooked, drain it in a colander, reserving the milk and the garlic but discarding the onion, peppercorns and bay. Push the potato through a sieve or mash well before transferring it to a bowl. Purée the salt cod in a food processor, along with the poached garlic, 50ml of the hot milk, and the olive oil, and then add it to the potato. Mix well and taste for seasoning (you may want to add a little more milk if the brandada seems stiff).

Serve warm, with a drizzle of olive oil on top, plus 1 teaspoon of avruga caviar, some chives and a few strips of piquillo pepper on each portion and plenty of toast on the side.

Mussels stuffed with pine nut pilav

Pilavs, unlike paellas or risottos, shouldn't be *al dente* but cooked through in a luxurious kind of way. In this dish, the mussels and pine nuts give additional textures on the tongue. It is usually eaten as part of a mezze but we like to serve it with cacik as a starter or main meal, or to accompany white fish. Cacik can be a dip or a soup (see page 11). Dill and cucumbers grow very well in the summer, and home-grown cucumbers have a particularly good flavour compared to shop-bought ones.

Serves 6

2kg mussels

3 tablespoons olive oil

75g unsalted butter

1 medium onion, finely chopped

$1/3$ teaspoon ground allspice

80g pine nuts

a medium bunch (25–30g) of dill, chopped

60g currants, soaked in warm water until plump

200g basmati rice, rinsed 3 times, then soaked in tepid salted water for 2 hours

Cacik as a dip

$1/2$ garlic clove, crushed to a paste with a pinch of salt

1 large cucumber, partly peeled and finely grated

$1/2$ tablespoon chopped fresh mint

2 tablespoons chopped fresh dill

200g good-quality Greek yoghurt, such as Total

To serve

a few sprigs of dill

$1/2$ teaspoon dried Turkish (mild) chilli flakes

1 lemon, cut into sixths

First prepare the mussels: wash them well, discarding any open ones that don't close when tapped on the work surface. Remove their beards and scrape off any barnacles. Heat the oil in a large saucepan over a high heat. Add the mussels, cover the pan and steam them, shaking the pan often, for 3–4 minutes, until they open (throw away any that remain closed). Drain the

mussels and reserve the cooking juices – measure out 350ml of the liquid (you may need to add a little water if there is not enough) and set aside. When the mussels are cool enough to handle, remove them from their shells without breaking the two halves of the shells apart. Reserve both the mussels and their shells.

Now make the pilav. Heat the butter in a medium saucepan until it foams. Add the onion and a pinch of salt and fry gently, stirring occasionally, for 10–15 minutes, until golden. Add the allspice, pine nuts and half the dill and fry for a minute. Now add the drained currants and rice and stir around for 30 seconds to coat everything in the butter. Pour in the mussel juice, cover with a circle of greaseproof paper and a tight-fitting lid and cook over a high heat for 5 minutes. Reduce the heat to medium–low and cook for another 5 minutes, then remove from the heat. Leave to rest, covered, for 5 minutes.

To make the cacik, stir the garlic, grated cucumber and herbs into the yoghurt. Season with salt and pepper to taste, plus a little water if necessary to get a spooning consistency.

Fold the mussel meat and the remaining dill into the cooked pilav and taste for seasoning. Use a spoon to stuff this mixture back into the reserved mussel shells (you will not need all the shells), then arrange on a plate with the sprigs of dill and Turkish chilli flakes on top. Serve with the cacik and lemon wedges on the side. This makes for delicious, but messy, finger food.

Meat Starters

Raw broad beans with jamón

We came across this celebration of the first harvest of young broad beans in Tuscany, sitting down to a huge pile of beans in their pods in the centre of the table accompanied by a young pecorino cheese. A couple of years later, we were thrilled to discover this tradition is also upheld in Spain. Thin slices of the highest-quality Joselito jamón ibérico were served as the accompaniment. We can't think of any better spring or early-summer lunch than chatting while podding the sweet young beans and eating them with mouthfuls of jamón and a glass of cold fino. To serve 4, you will need about 1.5kg young broad beans in their pods and 200g very thinly sliced jamón ibérico.

Kidneys with morel mushrooms and cinnamon yoghurt

Farika, the green roasted wheat from Lebanon, would be a strong contender for our desert island luxury. Morels are the best of the few wild mushrooms that appear in the spring; at any other time, dried morels make a perfectly good substitute. These two delicacies, combined with kidneys, make for one of our favourite starters. If accompanied by a green salad you can have an equally successful main course.

Serves 4

6 lamb's kidneys or 1 calf's kidney	2 tablespoons whole flat-leaf parsley
4 tablespoons olive oil	2 tablespoons chopped fresh tarragon

Farika

100g farika (or pearl barley)	6 allspice berries, crushed
25g unsalted butter	300ml light chicken stock, hot
4cm piece of cinnamon stick	

Morels

120–150g fresh morel mushrooms, or 30g dried morels just covered in boiling water	$1/2$ garlic clove, thinly sliced
	2 tablespoons olive oil

Cinnamon yoghurt

4 tablespoons good-quality Greek yoghurt, such as Total	2 tablespoons water
	a pinch of ground cinnamon

If using lamb's kidneys, slice them in half lengthways. If they are encased in their hard white fat (suet), simply remove it and peel off the thin membrane. Now, with scissors or a very sharp knife, snip out as much of the white gristle as possible, without cutting away any of the flesh. Then slice each half into bite-sized pieces – either halves or thirds, depending on the size of the kidney. For the calf's kidney, remove the suet and membrane from the whole kidney, then cut the kidney more or less according to its natural divisions.

Again, cut away any gristle and make sure all the pieces are approximately the same size so they cook evenly.

To prepare the farika, wash in a fine-meshed sieve to rinse off any dust or dirt, then leave to drain. Melt the butter with the cinnamon stick and allspice in a medium saucepan and, when it begins to foam and smell nutty, stir in the farika, followed by the hot stock. Place a circle of greaseproof paper over the farika, cover with a lid and simmer gently over the lowest possible heat for about 15–20 minutes, until the farika no longer has too much bite. Remove from the heat, season and set aside with the lid on to keep warm. (If using pearl barley, it can be cooked in the same way.)

Trim the ends of the fresh morels, then fill a sink with cold water, add the morels and toss for a minute to remove the grit. If they are still dirty, rinse one more time. Leave to drain thoroughly in a colander. If using dried morels, lift them out of the soaking liquid so as not to disturb any grit that might have settled at the bottom of the bowl, and squeeze out excess liquid. Cut any large mushrooms into halves or thirds. Fry the garlic in the olive oil over a medium heat until it colours, then add the fresh or dried morels and sauté for a couple of minutes. If using dried morels, pour in their soaking liquid through a fine-mesh sieve and simmer until just a couple of tablespoons of concentrated juice remain in the pan. Fresh morels should release their own juices while they cook. Season lightly.

For the cinnamon yoghurt, mix all the ingredients together and season with salt and pepper.

When you are ready to serve the dish, season the kidneys with a little salt and pepper and place a large frying pan over a high heat. When hot, add the olive oil and place the kidneys, cut-side up, in the pan. Fry for a minute or two until browned, then turn over to seal the other sides. Just before the kidneys are ready, stir in the morels and their juices. When cooked (the kidneys should still be pink and juicy inside), add the parsley and half the tarragon.

Lay the farika on 4 plates and put the kidneys and mushrooms on top. Spoon the yoghurt over the dish. Sprinkle with the remaining tarragon and serve immediately.

Chopped liver with paprika and cumin

This dish was inspired by a trip to Al Fna, the main square in Marrakech. As we sat down to a plate of merguez sausages, we noticed what looked like plump pincushions, sizzling furiously on the griddle. They turned out to be spiced stuffed spleen, which, when cooked, is chopped and eaten with bread. In the restaurant we use calf's liver and serve it with a wilted herb salad. We used to make a version of this warm salad when Moro first opened but the flavours were a bit strong and the idea sounded nicer than it tasted. Over the years we have learned that it should be made from herbs and foraged leaves that start to emerge in the spring, for that elusive, subtle taste. A little bit of everything makes the best wilted salad: handfuls of soft mallow, sweet, earthy chickweed and young nettle tops, peppery rocket and poppy leaves, bitter dandelion and lemony sorrel, as well as chard, parsley and coriander. The allotment is perfect for this, not only because of the abundance of these wild leaves, which grow freely on the verges, but also because you can grow as many herbs as you like. No more overpriced 15g packets, but rows of parsley, sorrel, mint and coriander that simply thrive when you pick them, so you come home with armfuls and can be as extravagant with them as you wish. The house always smells wonderful, too. We serve this dish with bread and occasionally yoghurt, although the latter is not especially traditional.

Serves 4

300g calf's or lamb's liver, thickly
    sliced
6 tablespoons olive oil

1 large Spanish onion, finely chopped
$3/4$ teaspoon freshly ground cumin

Wilted herb salad

3 tablespoons olive oil
1 garlic clove, thinly sliced
250g herbs – use 100g strongly
    flavoured mixed leaves (any or
    all of coriander, rocket,
    nasturtium and dandelion) and

150g milder leaves (any or all of
    young chard, spinach, mallow,
    rocket, parsley, sorrel, poppy,
    chickweed, nettletops), all washed
    and roughly chopped

To serve

a good pinch of sweet paprika

$1/2$ teaspoon ground cumin

$1/2$ heaped teaspoon Maldon sea salt

1 quantity of Flatbread (see page
    80), or 4 pitta breads

150g good-quality Greek yoghurt,
    such as Total, seasoned with a
    little salt and pepper (optional)

To prepare the liver, cut it into strips about 4–5cm long and 1.5cm wide, removing any veins as you go. Set aside.

Place a large frying pan over a medium heat and add 4 tablespoons of the olive oil. When it is hot, add the onion and a pinch of salt and turn the heat to low. Fry for 15–20 minutes, stirring often, until the onion has softened and is golden and sweet. Remove from the heat, scrape the onion and its oil into a bowl and set aside. You can use the frying pan again for the liver, without washing it.

While the onion is cooking, make the wilted herb salad. Heat the oil in a large saucepan over a medium heat, then add the garlic. Fry until the garlic begins to turn golden, then add the chopped leaves and a pinch of salt. Fry for a few minutes, stirring occasionally, until the leaves have wilted and are tender. Remove from the heat, taste for seasoning and keep warm.

When you are ready to cook the liver, place the frying pan over a medium to high heat and add the remaining 2 tablespoons of olive oil. When the oil is hot but not smoking, season the liver all over with the cumin and some salt and pepper and fry quickly on one side for about 1 minute, until sealed. Turn over and sear the other side. After another minute, when the liver is nicely coloured and just firm to the touch, return the onion mixture to the pan and stir it around. The liver should still be pink and juicy in the middle – test a piece, then transfer the rest to a chopping board. Chop the liver finely with the onion and taste for seasoning (you may want to add a touch of oil if it seems at all dry). Place them directly on the warm wilted herb salad.

Mix together the paprika, cumin and salt and sprinkle them over the liver. Serve immediately, with the bread and some yoghurt, if using.

Sweetbreads with prawns, girolles and oloroso sherry

This dish is Catalan in origin, with its *mar y tierra* marriage of ingredients from 'sea and land'. The Catalans are passionate about wild mushrooms, as are we. We have yet to find girolle mushrooms growing in London but instead we head for the Scottish Highlands where, from late summer to mid-autumn, you are more than likely to stumble across them in silver birch forests.

Serves 4

400g lamb's or calf's sweetbreads

$^1/_2$ lemon

4 tablespoons olive oil

$^1/_2$ garlic clove, thinly sliced

200g girolles or pieds de mouton, cleaned

50ml oloroso sherry

50ml water

300g cooked, shell-on North Atlantic prawns, peeled

2 tablespoons finely chopped fresh flat-leaf parsley

4 thick slices of rustic bread, toasted and drizzled with extra virgin olive oil

Rinse the sweetbreads in a colander under cold water for a minute or so, then place in a saucepan with the lemon and a little salt, cover with water and bring to the boil. Simmer gently for about 10–15 minutes, until just firm to the touch. Cool in their cooking liquid (add ice), then drain. Pick off and discard the outer membrane and any veins or fat. If using calf's sweetbreads, slice into 1cm-thick medallions. The lamb's sweetbreads are smaller, so do not need slicing, just breaking into bite-sized pieces. Blot the sweetbreads dry before using.

Place a wide frying pan over a medium-high heat and pour in the olive oil. Season the sweetbreads with salt and pepper. When the oil is hot, lay the sweetbreads in the pan. Fry until crisp and golden on the first side, then turn over to cook the other, tucking the garlic and girolles in between. Once the garlic has started to brown, toss the mushrooms and sweetbreads around with a spoon. After a few minutes, when the mushrooms are nearly done, add the sherry and water and let them bubble for a minute or two until you have a nice sauce. Add the prawns and parsley just to warm through. Taste for seasoning and serve on the toast.

Jamón with quail's eggs and piquillo peppers

We first had this tapa, a posh 'ham and eggs', in Granada. A piece of toast topped with a miniature fried egg, crisp and frilly round the edges from being fried in hot olive oil. The sweet fried pepper serves as a marvellous foil for both the egg and jamón, bringing all the flavours together.

We are often disappointed by the peppers on offer in the UK, and the allotment is a perfect way to experiment with more exciting varieties. Last year we grew the famous miniature green pimientos de Padrón from Galicia (one in ten blows your head off), piquillos from Navarra and 'goat's horn' from Andalucía, simply by collecting the seeds at the restaurant and planting them.

Serves 4

olive oil

6 tinned piquillo peppers, halved

8 quail's eggs

150g sliced best-quality jamón ibérico or prosciutto

4 slices of warm toast, gently rubbed with garlic and drizzled with olive oil

$1/2$ teaspoon ground cumin

Heat 3 tablespoons of olive oil in a frying pan, add the peppers and fry until lightly coloured in places. Remove from the heat and set aside.

Place a large frying pan over a medium to high heat and add 1mm depth of olive oil. When the oil is hot but not smoking, add the quail's eggs one by one. Cracking a quail's egg is quite fiddly and the shell thin, so it is easier to break each one into a little bowl beforehand, then gently slip them into the oil. They are ready when the whites are just opaque and slightly crisp round the edges but the yolks are still soft. Remove with a spatula and serve with the piquillo peppers and jamón, all three arranged on the toast or with the toast on the side. Finally sprinkle the eggs with the cumin and a little salt and pepper.

Kibbeh nayyeh

There are many kibbeh dishes, mostly made of lamb, some with pumpkin or spinach, but the one thing they have in common is that fine bulgur is kneaded into the mix to bind it. This Lebanese equivalent of steak tartare is delicately spiced with allspice and cinnamon and served with a basket of herbs and vegetables straight out of the allotment.

Serves 4

250g lamb fillet, trimmed of fat
    and sinew
75g fine bulgur
5 allspice berries, crushed
$^1/_4$ rounded teaspoon ground
    cinnamon

1 spring onion, very finely chopped
1 tablespoon finely chopped mild
    red chilli
1 tablespoon finely chopped fresh
    mint
4–5 tablespoons iced water

To serve

2 tablespoons extra virgin olive oil
20g pine nuts, toasted until golden
a bunch of radishes (with the leaves
    if they look nice)
a bunch of sweet cherry tomatoes
    straight from the plant
a few sprigs of savory, mint,
    coriander and/or tarragon

lemon wedges
8 pickled chillies
1 head of white chicory, leaves
    separated
warm Flatbread (see page 80) or
    lavash

Thinly slice the lamb fillet and then pulse it in a food processor until it turns into a paste.

Rinse the bulgur, place in a bowl and add a little water – just to the level of the surface of the wheat. Leave to soak for approximately 5 minutes, until it is quite *al dente* and the water has been absorbed. Combine the bulgur with the lamb, spices, spring onion, chilli and mint and knead well, as you would knead bread dough, until everything is evenly combined. Add the water a spoonful at a time (this is to re-moisten the mix, as the bulgur will absorb moisture from the lamb). Season with salt and pepper and leave in the refrigerator for 20–30 minutes.

Spread the kibbeh flat on a plate, drizzle with the olive oil and sprinkle with the pine nuts. Serve with the radishes, tomatoes, fresh herbs, lemon wedges and pickled chillies on the side and use the chicory leaves and warm flatbread or lavash to scoop up the lamb.

Smoked duck breast with apples, walnuts and chicory

In Catalunya ducks and geese are an important part of the food psyche. It is a marked link between the Spanish and their French cousins. Jamón de pato, or smoked duck breast, is quite expensive and not that easy to get hold of, so at Moro we hot-smoke our own, using sawdust or wood chippings. It is surprisingly easy to over-smoke the breast, so be warned. To accompany the duck, we serve an autumnal, bitter-sweet salad.

Serves 4

2 duck breasts
1 small garlic clove
2 teaspoons fresh thyme leaves
2 cloves

500g coarse sea salt or Maldon salt
30–40g fine wood chips or shavings
10g fresh rosemary, roughly chopped
1 tablespoon water

Dressing

$^1/_2$ garlic clove, crushed to a paste with a pinch of salt

1 tablespoon sherry vinegar (or good-quality red wine vinegar)
4 tablespoons olive oil

Salad

100g frisée salad (pale leaves only)
2 heads of white or green chicory, trimmed of any damaged leaves and cut across into 3cm slices
2 small apples, such as Coxes or Braeburns, cut in half, cored and thinly sliced (do this just before serving, lest they turn brown)

1 small bunch (about 20g) of flat-leaf parsley, leaves picked
50g walnuts
50g raisins, soaked in warm water until plump

First, cure and smoke the duck breasts. Crush the garlic, thyme and cloves to a paste with $^1/_2$ teaspoon salt and some pepper. Rub this paste on the fleshy side of the breasts. Put half the salt in a colander, lay the breasts flesh-side down on top and cover with the remaining salt. Leave to cure in a cool place or in the fridge for 16–20 hours.

The next day, shake off as much salt as possible and rinse the duck under cold running water. Blot dry with kitchen paper and place skin-side down in a heavy frying pan. Put the pan over a very low heat for 15–20 minutes to render the fat slowly without cooking the meat. Remove and blot dry once the skin starts to colour.

Mix the wood chips and rosemary together and moisten with the water. Make a pile in one corner of the widest frying pan you can find, then place this corner over a high heat. You need to heat the wood chips until they start to smoke and burn without making the rest of the pan too hot, so use the smallest hob on its highest setting to control the heat. As the wood starts to smoke heavily, place the duck breasts, skin-side down, in the opposite corner of the pan. Cover with a tight-fitting lid or aluminium foil and smoke for 6 minutes, still leaving the side of the pan containing the wood chips over a high heat. Turn off the heat, remove the duck from the pan and leave to cool. Chill slightly before serving. You can do all this in advance.

Make the dressing by whisking together the garlic, vinegar and oil and season with salt and pepper. To assemble the salad, place the frisée, chicory, apples, whole parsley leaves, walnuts and raisins in a salad bowl. Toss well with the dressing and some salt and pepper, then arrange on serving plates. Now slice the duck breasts very thinly across the grain and place on top of the salad.

Duck liver terrine with grapes

This terrine is perhaps a bit grand for the allotment but when the grapes ripen – and, believe it or not, there are many vines in Hackney Wick – it is a must. At Moro we use Catalan foie gras drizzled with arrope – a sweet, sticky molasses made from grape must, which we buy from one of our Spanish suppliers, Sayell Foods. You can replace this by reducing some oloroso, or Pedro Ximénez sherry or muscatel wine. And if you want to go for the whole sherry experience, serve the terrine with a glass of oloroso.

Serves 8

1 whole, fresh raw duck or goose foie gras (liver), about 600–700g in weight

100ml medium oloroso sherry

1/2 garlic clove, crushed to a smooth paste with a pinch of salt

40g unsalted butter

20 large muscat grapes, cut in half and pips removed

200g mâche salad

2 tablespoons extra virgin olive oil

a squeeze of lemon

To serve

8 tablespoons (120ml) arrope (or 360ml muscatel, or oloroso or Pedro Ximénez sherry, boiled until reduced by two-thirds to make a thick syrup)

1 teaspoon sherry vinegar or red wine vinegar

Maldon sea salt

The terrine should be made a day in advance. Cut the foie (liver) into slices 1.5cm thick, removing any large veins. Marinate it in the oloroso and crushed garlic for 6 hours or overnight.

Drain the liver, discarding the marinade, and season with a little salt and pepper. Line a small terrine (about 1 litre in capacity) with cling film. Place a frying pan over a medium to high heat and when it is quite hot add the slices of foie gras. They will release plenty of fat, so there is no need to add any oil. After 1 minute or less when the first side is coloured, turn each slice over to cook the other. When done, the foie will be soft in the middle and browned on both sides. Lay the warm slices in the terrine and pour over the fat that has been rendered in the pan. Press the foie down gently so the fat rests on top. Allow to cool slightly, then put it in the fridge overnight to set.

To serve, turn out the terrine, cut 8 thick slices and lay them on individual plates. Heat the butter in a frying pan and, when it begins to foam and caramelise, add the grapes, cut-side down. Season with a touch of salt, fry for a minute, then turn them over. While the grapes are cooking, dress the mâche salad with the olive oil, lemon juice and some salt and pepper. Mix the arrope with the vinegar.

Put the salad on the serving plates next to the terrine. Spoon the grapes over the salad, drizzle the arrope on top of each slice of terrine and sprinkle with a little Maldon salt. Serve with plenty of toast on the side.

Morteruelo de Cuenca

This warm hare and partridge pâté is good, rich country fare that comes from the region of Castilla-La Mancha. It is the sort of thing Don Quixote might have munched on at a roadside *venta*. Traditionally a little pig's liver goes into this dish, but we find incorporating the hare or rabbit liver enough.

You can make it two or three days in advance, and it will even improve over this time. In Spain it would be accompanied by regaña, hard crackers that are served with tapas. Carr's water biscuits work very well, as does toast. We haven't heard of anyone shooting the odd rabbit or hare on the allotment, but this recipe makes good use of the hardy herbs that grow so well up there, requiring absolutely no attention.

Serves 4–6

6 tablespoons olive oil

$^1/_2$ small hare or 1 small wild rabbit, jointed into 5 pieces (keep the liver)

1 partridge or $^1/_2$ pheasant, split in half

1 medium onion, finely chopped

3 garlic cloves, thinly sliced

150g pancetta or smoked streaky bacon, trimmed and cut into matchsticks

100g tocino or lardo (the Italian equivalent), good-quality lard from the butcher, or jamón fat

$^1/_2$ teaspoon dried oregano

a few sprigs of thyme, tied in a bundle

2 bay leaves, preferably fresh

2 cloves, crushed

$^1/_2$ teaspoon ground cinnamon

$^3/_4$ teaspoon sweet paprika

150ml sweet sherry (medium/sweet oloroso, cream or Pedro Ximénez)

1 litre water

3 tablespoons dried breadcrumbs

To serve

4 teaspoons lightly toasted pine nuts

a sprinkling of sweet paprika, smoked or unsmoked

100g watercress, dressed with a squeeze of lemon and extra virgin olive oil

crackers or toast

Preheat the oven to 200°C/400°F/Gas 6.

Heat the olive oil in a large casserole and brown the game, including the liver, in batches. Put the game to one side. Fry the onion, garlic, pancetta and tocino all together for 20 minutes or until everything is starting to brown. Add the herbs and spices and cook for a couple more minutes. Add the sherry and water and return the game to the pot. Bring to a simmer, skimming off any scum that appears. Cover with greaseproof paper, followed by a lid or foil, and put in the oven for $2-2^1/_2$ hours, turning the meat after $1-1^1/_2$ hours. When it is done, the meat should be falling off the bone.

Strain the gravy, reserving the bits of onion and pancetta. Taste and if the flavour isn't strong enough, boil until reduced to about 400ml of strong, flavoursome broth. Stir in the breadcrumbs.

Pick the meat off the bones, shredding it as you go (take care: a hare or rabbit bone can be sharp if splintered). Go through the onion and pancetta bits to make sure there are no bones hiding, then add them to the meat. Mash vigorously with your hands until quite smooth. Stir in the gravy and season with salt and pepper as required. The consistency should be that of a dip (thin with water or thicken with breadcrumbs as required). Serve warm, with the pine nuts and a bit of paprika sprinkled on top, accompanied by the dressed watercress, crackers, toast or bread.

Partridge escabeche

Partridge escabeche is a dish that has been enjoyed in Andalucía for centuries. The meat takes on the subtle flavour of the fragrant vinegar, and is delicious shredded on salads or eaten warm with boiled potatoes and braised cabbage or spinach. It makes an interesting alternative to the braised or roast partridge more usually served in British kitchens.

Serves 4 as a starter, 2 as a main course

2 partridges
2 tablespoons olive oil

Escabeche marinade

1 small red onion, thinly sliced	2 teaspoons coriander seeds
8 tablespoons (120ml) sherry vinegar	1 teaspoon black peppercorns
8 tablespoons (120ml) sweet red wine vinegar, such as Forum (or use balsamic vinegar)	a few parsley stalks (optional)
	1 teaspoon sugar
	4 fresh bay leaves
1 dried guindilla chilli pepper, seeded and thinly sliced, or $1/2$ teaspoon hot paprika	2 teaspoons fine sea salt
	300ml water

Season the partridges with a little salt and pepper, then brown them on all sides in the olive oil over a medium heat, paying particular attention to the breasts. The birds should be beautifully brown and nearly cooked (perhaps medium-rare) when they are ready – around 15 minutes in all. Put them breast-side down in a non-reactive plastic, glass, ceramic or stainless-steel container (not enamel or aluminium) in which they fit snugly.

Put all the marinade ingredients in a pan, bring to the boil and pour immediately over the partridges. Allow to cool for a few hours before covering and putting in the fridge. The next day, or up to 3 days later, they are good to eat.

If you want to serve the partridges cold, as a starter, take them out of the fridge and bring to room temperature, then take the breast meat off the bones and tear it into largish chunks. It is very good served on a salad of chicory dressed with olive oil and red wine vinegar, with a tablespoon or so of the onion in the marinade strewn on top of the partridge and a handful of walnuts scattered over.

To eat the birds hot, as a main course, place them in a small saucepan and pour over the marinade to cover. Leave over a medium heat, until the meat is thoroughly hot, but don't let the liquid boil.

Braised kale with chicharrones

At the restaurant, if we are taking the rind off a pork loin so as to braise it or make albóndigas (meatballs), we put chicharrones on the menu. Chicharrones are a naughty but delectable tapa – pork rinds that have been salted, spiced and roasted until highly crispy. (Yes, pork scratchings!) We decided they would be particularly good served on greens – kale, turnip tops (*grelos*), rape tops or mustard tops. The last two are generally recognisable by the vast fields of yellow one sees around England in the summer, but if picked young, when the flowerheads have not yet opened, they can be eaten like sprouting broccoli and are a real treat.

If you don't want to make chicharrones, then fried chorizo is also delicious in this dish. We have given recipes for both, so you decide.

Serves 4

600g kale, rape, mustard greens, turnip tops, or winter cabbage, stalks removed

4 tablespoons olive oil
1 garlic clove, thinly sliced
1–2 tablespoons sherry vinegar

Chicharrones

$1/_4$ teaspoon cumin seeds
$1/_4$ teaspoon fennel seeds
$1/_4$ teaspoon coriander seeds
$1/_4$ teaspoon sweet paprika, preferably smoked

1 teaspoon fine sea salt
350g pork skin, cut in 5 x 1cm strips

Chorizo

1 tablespoon olive oil

200g chorizo (uncured if possible, cut in rounds 1cm thick)

Preheat the oven to 230°C/450°F/Gas 8.

For the chicharrones, grind the spices with the salt, then toss the strips of skin in the spice mix. Spread out evenly on a baking sheet and roast for 10–15 minutes, until light, bubbly and golden brown. Check the cracklings as they cook, removing any that are ready before the rest, lest they burn.

Alternatively for the chorizo, place a frying pan over a medium-high heat and add the olive oil. Fry the chorizo slices for a minute or two on each side, until slightly crisp. Set aside and keep warm.

Blanch the greens in plenty of boiling salted water for a couple of minutes, until just tender, then refresh under cold running water and squeeze dry. Now place a frying pan over a medium heat and add the olive oil. When hot, add the garlic and fry until just golden, then add the greens and a pinch of salt. Stir well and sauté until the greens are warm. Add the sherry vinegar to taste and check the seasoning. Transfer to a plate and serve with the hot chicharrones or chorizo (with the red pan juices) on top – or with both! Eat immediately.

Salads

Reg's allotment salad

The point of this dish is to gather whatever you have ready in the garden to make a delicious salad; it uses so many ingredients that it can be a great way for a number of allotment neighbours to pool their resources.

Reg is a handsome man of few words, in his seventies. Being of few words is useful when preparing a salad as time-consuming as this. It is a real labour of love and a joy to eat, either on its own or as an accompaniment to grilled chicken or lamb. Thank you, Reg!

Serves 6–8

2 garlic cloves (new season's, if possible), finely chopped
1 Cos lettuce, outer leaves removed, finely shredded
1 small new season's onion or 2 spring onions, sliced into thin rings (all the green part, too)
1 small red onion, finely chopped
1 large or 2 small raw beetroot, grated
2 carrots, grated
2 handfuls of purslane, roughly chopped
12 cherry tomatoes, cut into quarters, or 2–3 large tomatoes, chopped

10 radishes, trimmed and sliced thinly
1 large cucumber, peeled, quartered lengthways and thinly sliced
1 medium kohlrabi, cut into matchsticks
1 green pepper, finely chopped
1–2 fresh chillies, if you like a little heat, cut in half lengthways, seeded and finely chopped
1 small fennel bulb and its tops, finely chopped
2 handfuls of sorrel, shredded
3 tablespoons roughly chopped fresh flat-leaf parsley
1 heaped tablespoon finely chopped fresh mint

Dressing

7 tablespoons (105ml) extra virgin olive oil

juice of $^1/_2$ lemon or 1–2 tablespoons red wine vinegar

Put everything in a large salad bowl. Pour over the oil and lemon juice or vinegar and season with salt and pepper. The salad may have a purple/red hue from the beetroot.

Chopped green salad

One Sunday we were invited by Adile to her allotment for kebabs. When we say kebabs, we also mean grilled green chillies and tomatoes, a basketful of herbs and spring onions, yoghurt and warm, thin pitta bread – a typical allotment feast. We also ate a lemony chopped salad of chard, sorrel, rocket and onion tops, which cut through the fatty, delicately spiced kebab. The moment our plates were empty, we were offered more until we had to be firm in our refusal. Such is the generosity of our friends.

Serves 4–6

100g sorrel leaves
100g tender young chard or spinach
   leaves, stalks removed
50g onion tops or 2 spring onions,
   thinly sliced

50g rocket
3 tablespoons extra virgin olive oil
1 dessertspoon lemon juice

Make sure all the leaves are washed and dried, then shred them into 5mm strips and dress with the olive oil, lemon juice and some salt and pepper. Serve immediately.

Beetroot and broad bean salad

The combination of beetroot and tarragon is a winner and, since it is one of our favourite herbs, we always make sure we grow a lot of tarragon on the allotment. There is nothing we like more than stuffing handfuls of the herb inside a chicken for roasting, so the flavour really comes through.

Serves 4

500g beetroot, young if possible,
   skin on, scrubbed to remove dirt
300g podded new season's broad
   beans, preferably small

4 tablespoons extra virgin olive oil
1 tablespoon good red wine vinegar,
   with $1/2$ teaspoon sugar if very
   acidic

2 spring onions, thinly sliced   a medium bunch (about 20g) of
                                        tarragon, leaves picked

First boil the beetroot in plenty of salted water until tender in the middle –
this will take about 1–2 hours, depending on size. Drain and peel under
running water whilst still warm, then set aside. While the beetroot are cooking, boil the broad beans in unsalted water until just tender, then drain and
refresh under cold water and drain once more. Peel any broad beans that are
larger than your thumbnail.

     Make a dressing by mixing the oil and vinegar together, then season
with salt and pepper. Slice the beetroot in half and then into wedges about
5mm thick and place in a mixing bowl. Pour over the dressing, season with a
little salt and pepper and toss. Now add the broad beans, spring onions and
half the tarragon and toss again. Transfer to a dish and put the remaining
tarragon on top. Serve immediately.

Broad bean, tomato and anchovies with fresh cheese

We have never grown broad beans late enough or tomatoes early enough to be able to make this salad entirely from the allotment. When we make it at the restaurant in June, we use Sicilian cherry tomatoes and organically grown English broad beans.

Serves 4

150g podded young broad beans
8–12 cherry tomatoes, cut into
    halves or quarters, depending on
    size
1 spring onion, thinly sliced
6 tablespoons extra virgin olive oil
1 dessertspoon lemon juice

150g soft fresh curd cheese (page 283)
    or ricotta cheese
4 salted anchovy fillets, cut in half
    lengthways
1 tablespoon finely shredded fresh
    mint
zest of $\frac{1}{2}$ lemon

Blanch the broad beans in a pan of boiling unsalted water for 4–8 minutes, until tender, then drain. Peel any that are larger than your thumbnail. Place the broad beans, tomatoes and spring onion in a bowl and dress with 4 table-spoons of the oil, the lemon juice and some salt and pepper. Spread out on a large plate, dot 4 dollops of curd cheese with 2 anchovy strips in a cross on top of each, followed by the shredded mint, lemon zest and a little black pepper. Drizzle with the remaining olive oil and serve immediately.

Radish, kohlrabi and mooli salad

This crunchy salad uses ordinary red radishes, kohlrabi (one of Hassan's favourite crops) and mooli (white radish, or daikon). If you don't grow your own, you are most likely to find them in Turkish shops. Each variety has its own sweetness and spiciness, so a mixture makes an otherwise ordinary radish salad subtle and interesting. This one makes a delicious accompaniment to fish and/or a pilav.

Serves 4

8 radishes (about 150g), thinly sliced
1 small to medium kohlrabi (about 250g), peeled, quartered and thinly sliced
250g mooli (daikon), peeled, halved lengthways and thinly sliced
2 tablespoons finely chopped fresh mint

1 dessertspoon black onion seeds
$1/2$ teaspoon dried Turkish (mild) chilli flakes (optional)
$1/2$ teaspoon orange blossom water (optional)

Dressing

4 tablespoons extra virgin olive oil
juice of $1/2$ lemon

$1/2$ small garlic clove, crushed to a paste with a pinch of salt

To make the dressing, whisk the oil, lemon juice and garlic together until more or less emulsified and season with salt and pepper.

To assemble the salad, place all the ingredients in a mixing bowl. Pour over the dressing, toss and check for seasoning. Eat immediately, or the vegetables will lose their crunch.

Allotment herb salad

Use whichever of the herbs listed below you have available. At times of plenty, this will make a large and varied salad. When there is less available in the garden, just increase the quantities of whatever you do have, or supplement your produce with a little help from the greengrocer. Serve the salad with a couple of good cheeses and fresh bread.

Serves 4

1 handful each of tarragon, chervil, chives, basil, mint, dill, nasturtium leaf

$^1/_2$ handful of oregano or marjoram

2 handfuls of rocket, parsley, young chard, spinach or beet leaves, sorrel and fennel

2 spring onions, thinly sliced

petals from 3 heads of calendula (marigold) and a handful of borage flowers and/or nasturtium flowers (visually the flowers make a real difference, so are worth finding)

Dressing

1 tablespoon red wine vinegar

a tiny squeeze of lemon

4 tablespoons extra virgin olive oil

Whisk all the dressing ingredients together and season with salt and pepper. Place all the leaves, onions and petals in a large salad bowl. Pour over the dressing and check once more for seasoning.

Grilled onion salad with yoghurt

We are very fond of this salad – velvety, sweet and smoky onions coated in yoghurt. It is quite a combination and goes well with grilled meat or fish. If you have access to home-grown or new season's onions from late spring, you are in for an especially tasty treat.

Serves 4

1kg new season's onions with tops on, red onions or spring onions, roots trimmed

200g good-quality Greek yoghurt, such as Total, thinned to the texture of cream with 50–100ml water

2 tablespoons extra virgin olive oil

$1/4$ garlic clove, crushed with a pinch of salt

$1^1/2$ teaspoons fresh thyme leaves, lightly crushed

1–2 teaspoons zaatar (a Lebanese mix of summer savory, sumac and sesame) – see page 251

Place the whole onions over a hot barbecue, or directly on the naked flame of a gas hob or under the grill until the skin is charred and crisp all over and the flesh is very soft. This could take anything from 15–30 minutes, depending on the size of the onions.

Meanwhile, season the yoghurt with the olive oil, garlic and thyme, adding salt and pepper to taste.

When the onions are cool enough to handle, peel off any burnt skin, place the onions in a large mixing bowl, then pour the yoghurt over the top and mix well. Taste for seasoning and sprinkle with the zaatar.

Grilled onion, pepper and lentil salad

Once you have mastered the art of grilling onions (see page 133), try this combination, which is a little more elaborate. This salad was made for us by our friend Linn Lee.

Serves 4

175g small brown lentils
300g small new season's onions
    with tops on (or spring onions),
    roots trimmed

2 red peppers
1 small bunch (about 20g) of flat-
    leaf parsley, leaves picked and
    roughly chopped

Dressing
4 tablespoons extra virgin olive oil
1 tablespoon good-quality red wine
    vinegar with $^1/_2$ teaspoon sugar,
    or sherry or Pedro Ximenez vinegar

$^1/_2$ small garlic clove, crushed to a
    paste with a pinch of salt

To make the dressing, whisk all the ingredients together and season to taste with salt and pepper.

Put the lentils in a saucepan and cover generously with water. Bring to the boil, reduce the heat to a gentle simmer and cook for 15–20 minutes or until the lentils are just cooked but still firm, as it is important that they retain their shape. Remove from the heat, season with a little salt and set aside.

Grill the onions and peppers whole over a hot barbecue, or directly on the naked flame of a gas hob or under the grill, for 15–20 minutes, until the skin is charred and crisp all over and the flesh is very soft. Cover with cling film or place in a plastic bag to soften the skins. When cool enough to handle, pick any blackened skin off the onions and tear them into 5cm lengths. Peel and seed the peppers and tear them into strips, then put them in a large mixing bowl along with the onions and parsley. Drain the warm lentils, reserving 3–4 tablespoons of their liquid, and add them to the bowl with the reserved liquid and the dressing. Toss well and check for seasoning.

Ensalada piperada

This dish is similar to the Turkish chopped salad in our earlier book *Casa Moro*. Amalia, from the Hotel Berchules in the Alpujarras in Andalucía, prepared this dish to go alongside a plate of semolina Migas (see page 225), while elsewhere it is served with fried fish. The avocado brings added richness, but it can be made without it.

Serves 4

1 cucumber, peeled, cut into eighths
    lengthways and sliced across to
    make 5mm-thick triangles
3 tablespoons chopped red
    onion
1 small green pepper, seeded and
    chopped

16 sweet cherry tomatoes on the
    vine, chopped
1 ripe avocado, peeled, stoned
    and chopped (optional)

Dressing

1 garlic clove, crushed to a paste
    with a pinch of salt
3 tablespoons extra virgin olive oil

1 tablespoon red wine vinegar (add
    $1/2$ teaspoon sugar if the vinegar
    is overly sharp)

Whisk all the dressing ingredients together until more or less emulsified, seasoning with salt and pepper.

Place all the chopped ingredients in a salad bowl. Pour on the dressing, toss well and check for seasoning. Serve immediately.

Grilled aubergine salad with tomatoes and pomegranates

The combination of tomatoes, aubergines and pomegranates is typically Syrian. We have not had that much success with aubergines on the allotment, which may just need more of a Mediterranean climate, but we do have a pomegranate tree at home that has produced fruit two years running now, so there is hope!

Serves 4

3 medium aubergines (about 800g in total)

1 tablespoon tahini

200g ripe cherry tomatoes, cut into halves or quarters

2 spring onions, trimmed and thinly sliced

seeds of $^1/_2$ medium pomegranate (about 70g)

1 small bunch of mint (about 15g), roughly chopped

Dressing

juice of $^1/_2$ medium pomegranate (see page 52)

$^1/_2$ garlic clove, crushed to a paste with a pinch of salt

3 tablespoons extra virgin olive oil

For the dressing, whisk all the ingredients together, season with salt and pepper and set aside.

Grill the aubergines whole over a hot barbecue, or directly on the naked flame of a gas hob or under the grill, until the skin is charred and crisp all over and the flesh is very soft. If none of these options is available, prick the aubergines with a fork and place in a very hot oven at 220°C/425°F/Gas 7 for about 45–60 minutes, until soft. Remove from the heat.

When the aubergines are cool enough to handle, discard the tops and peel off the skin, scraping the flesh from the back of the skin if necessary. Chop the flesh roughly with a knife, then place in a large mixing bowl and mix by hand until almost smooth. Add the tahini and dressing and taste for seasoning. Now add the tomatoes, spring onions, pomegranate seeds and mint and stir well. Check for salt and pepper once more.

Tunisian pepper and tomato salad

The culinary accent of this salad is changed from Moroccan to Tunisian by the use of caraway and chilli instead of cumin and coriander. Hassan often gives us some of his surplus chilli seedlings, which we happily plant and they keep us going right through the autumn.

Serves 4

1 large red pepper

1 large yellow pepper

1 large red chilli

300g cherry tomatoes, halved

a small bunch (about 20g) of coriander, leaves picked

Dressing

$1/2$ teaspoon caraway seeds, crushed

$1/2$ teaspoon unsmoked paprika

$1/2$ teaspoon ground cumin

3 tablespoons extra virgin olive oil

1 teaspoon red wine vinegar

Place the red, yellow and chilli peppers whole over a hot barbecue, or directly on the naked flame of a gas hob or under the grill, until the skin is charred all over and the flesh is very soft. Put the blackened peppers into a plastic bag or a bowl covered with cling film to steam and loosen their skin. When cool enough to handle, peel and seed them. Tear the sweet peppers into strips, and chop the chilli finely.

In a large bowl, stir together the spices with the oil and vinegar to make the dressing, then season with salt and pepper. Add the peppers, tomatoes and coriander to the bowl and toss, then taste for seasoning.

Lentil, tomato and dill salad

Tomatoes and dill are a more unusual combination than basil or oregano, yet no lesser for it.

Serves 4

175g small brown lentils
200g ripe cherry tomatoes, cut into
   halves or quarters
$1/_2$ small red onion, thinly sliced
a small bunch (about 10g) of dill,
   coarsely chopped

5 tablespoons extra virgin olive oil
1 tablespoon lemon juice, or good-
   quality red wine vinegar with a
   pinch of sugar

Put the lentils in a saucepan and cover generously with water. Bring to the boil, reduce the heat to a gentle simmer and cook for 15–20 minutes, until they are just cooked, firm and definitely not soft, as it is important that they retain their shape. Remove from the heat, season with a little salt and drain, reserving 3–4 tablespoons of their liquid.

     Place the warm, drained lentils and reserved liquid in a mixing bowl, add the tomatoes, red onion and dill and dress with the olive oil, lemon juice or vinegar, and some salt and pepper.

Tomato, red onion and cumin salad

This is a very simple salad that we have tried to make as complicated as possible. Over-complicated recipes are a sin, yet sometimes when we cook at friends' houses they say, 'If I made that it wouldn't taste the same.' This is an example of how we would try to get the best out of such a simple thing.

Serves 4

1 medium red onion, peeled but
   left whole
300ml milk
4 ice cubes
1 rounded teaspoon cumin seeds
$1/2$ teaspoon black peppercorns

500–600g flavoursome tomatoes
a good pinch of Maldon sea salt
1 tablespoon flat-leaf parsley leaves
a good drizzle (about 50ml) of extra
   virgin olive oil

Slice the onion into rounds of medium thickness and put them in a bowl. Cover with the milk and add the ice cubes (the milk softens the astringent quality of the onions, while the ice crisps them up). Let them stand for 10–30 minutes.

Put the cumin seeds in a pan over a medium heat until they are noticeably darker. Crush roughly in a mortar and pestle; they should still be recognisable as cumin seeds. Set aside.

Now coarsely crush the pepper in the mortar and pestle. Slice the tomatoes and spread them out on a serving plate. Sprinkle the spices and salt evenly over the tomatoes, hardly crushing the salt at all. Allow to stand for 5 minutes.

Drain the onion and pat dry. Arrange the onion slices evenly over the tomatoes, followed by the parsley. Drizzle with olive oil and serve.

Beetroot salad with pistachio sauce

This is a pretty and fragrant salad. If you are not convinced by the youth/juiciness of your beetroot, we would recommend boiling them until just tender and slicing them before mixing with all the other ingredients.

Serves 4

500g raw young beetroot, peeled
    and very thinly sliced or grated
a small handful of flat-leaf parsley,
    leaves picked

2 teaspoons lemon juice
2 tablespoons extra virgin olive oil

Pistachio sauce

100g shelled unsalted pistachios
2 tablespoons finely chopped fresh
    flat-leaf parsley
1 dessertspoon finely chopped fresh
    mint
1 dessertspoon lemon juice
$1/2$ teaspoon caster sugar

7 tablespoons (105ml) extra virgin
    olive oil
$1/2$ teaspoon finely grated lemon zest
4 tablespoons water
$1/2$ teaspoon orange blossom water
    (optional)

To make the pistachio sauce, finely chop the pistachios by hand or in a food processor. Mix with all the other ingredients and season to taste with salt and pepper.

When you are ready to serve the salad, dress the beetroot and parsley leaves with the lemon juice and oil and season with salt and pepper. Spread out on a large platter and spoon the pistachio sauce over. Serve immediately.

Moroccan spiced potato salad

Potato salad we all know and love and when you combine it with a little heat and spices, it is transported to another realm.

Serves 4

1kg small–medium potatoes, such as Jersey Royal, Linzer Delikatess or Cyprus, skins on, scrubbed

1 large shallot, or 2 spring onions thinly sliced
1 small bunch (about 20g) of fresh coriander, leaves picked

Dressing

$1/_2$ garlic clove
$1/_2$ teaspoon salt
$1/_2$ teaspoon cumin seeds
$3/_4$ teaspoon caraway seeds

1 tablespoon lemon juice
2 tablespoons Harissa (see page 271)
4 tablespoons extra virgin olive oil

Put the potatoes in a pan with plenty of cold water and a hefty pinch of salt. Bring to a boil and cook until tender in the middle, then drain immediately. Leave, uncovered, until cool enough to handle.

While the potatoes are boiling, make the dressing. Pound the garlic, salt, cumin and caraway to a paste in a mortar and pestle, then stir in the lemon juice, harissa and olive oil. Taste for seasoning and set aside.

Peel the still-warm potatoes and slice them into rounds 1cm thick. Toss them with the shallot, coriander and spicy dressing and taste for seasoning.

Feta, chicory and orange salad

This salad is particularly good and colourful made with blood oranges when they are in season, from January onwards. A simpler version, omitting the feta and walnuts, makes a tasty side dish to accompany grilled fish and duck.

Serves 4

2 large oranges, or 3 blood oranges

3 heads of white chicory, any damaged outer leaves removed, whole leaves or sliced across into 2cm pieces

1 small bunch (about 20g) of flat-leaf parsley, leaves picked

1 tablespoon fresh oregano leaves, coarsely chopped if large

$1/2$ very small red onion, sliced as thinly as possible

100g good-quality feta cheese

150g walnut halves

50g oily black olives

Dressing

4 tablespoons extra virgin olive oil

1 tablespoon red wine vinegar, plus a pinch of caster sugar if the vinegar is very acidic

Whisk the dressing ingredients together until they have more or less emulsified, seasoning to taste with salt and pepper.

With a small sharp knife, preferably serrated, cut the rind and all the pith off the oranges, keeping the oranges whole. Now slice into 5mm–1cm rounds and place in a large salad or mixing bowl. Add the chicory, parsley, oregano and onion, pour on the dressing and gently toss together. Crumble the feta on top, then sprinkle over the walnuts and olives.

Bulgur, celery and pomegranate salad

A colourful, crunchy salad, great with fish, chicken or lamb, and another brilliant way to put the celery centre stage.

Serves 4

100g medium or coarse bulgur
400g celery (a small head), cut in 5mm slices on a slight bias – keep any young yellow leaves
seeds of $^1/_2$ large pomegranate (about 100g)

75g walnuts, roughly chopped
1 small bunch (about 20g) of flat-leaf parsley, coarsely chopped
1 scant tablespoon finely chopped fresh mint

Dressing
juice of $^1/_2$ large pomegranate (see page 52)

$^1/_2$ garlic clove, crushed to a paste with $^1/_2$ teaspoon of salt
6 tablespoons extra virgin olive oil

For the dressing, whisk all the ingredients together, season to taste with salt and pepper and set aside.

Put the bulgur in a bowl, add water to just below the surface of the wheat and leave it to stand for 10 minutes, until just tender but still quite *al dente*. Add more water as required or drain in a colander if at all wet.

Put all the ingredients in a bowl, pour over the dressing and check the seasoning. Serve immediately. Make sure the walnuts are dressed just before serving, as sometimes they can impart a bitter flavour and unpleasant colour to the dressing if left to sit.

Chard with chickpeas and tahini

Whilst we were testing recipes for this book, this dish was born as a result of not liking another one we were trying out. It was a Cos lettuce salad with white beans, boiled egg and olives dressed with tahini sauce. After several mouthfuls, we thought it wasn't quite right, and decided on this simpler but more delicious version, which is especially good with fish and chicken.

Chard is an excellent allotment vegetable to grow, as it keeps going throughout the year provided you look after it. We grow rainbow chard, which gets its name from the vibrant yellow, pink and white stalks.

Serves 4

600g chard, leaves and stalks (you
    will need less if it is very young,
    more if the leaves and stalks are
    big)
4 tablespoons extra virgin olive oil
2 squeezes of lemon
a 400g jar of good-quality cooked
    chickpeas (or 200g drained and
    seasoned cooked chickpeas)

1 quantity of Tahini Sauce (see
    page 265)
1 large red chilli, seeded and finely
    chopped
$1/2$ teaspoon black onion seeds
    (optional)

To prepare the chard, cut the leaves from the stalks and then cut the stalks into 5cm lengths. You need about 400g leaf and 100g stalk (you will probably have to discard some excess stalk). Bring a large pan of well-salted water to the boil and blanch the leaves in it for 1–2 minutes, until tender. Drain them, refresh under cold water and drain once more. Now blanch the stalks, which will take a few minutes longer than the leaves, then drain and refresh as before. Squeeze the chard dry.

When you are ready to serve, dress the chard with 2 tablespoons of the oil and a squeeze of lemon, plus some salt and pepper, and spread it out on a plate. Put the drained chickpeas in a saucepan with 4 tablespoons of water and the remaining oil and lemon and warm them gently. Stir the tahini sauce into the chickpeas and pour them over the chard. Sprinkle with the chopped chilli and black onion seeds (if using) before serving.

Macaroni and yoghurt salad

Pasta is used surprisingly frequently in North Africa, and especially in Libya where this salad hails from. At Moro we might serve this with fish or chicken, accompanied by a Tomato, red onion and cumin salad (page 143) or braised spinach. The spice we use at Moro is baharat (which simply means 'spice' in Arabic). It is a generic blend of spices that can vary from country to country. We use a blend of nutmeg, clove and cinnamon – 1:1:2.

Serves 4

200g macaroni

20g pine nuts

40g unsalted butter

200g good-quality Greek yoghurt, such as Total, thinned with 4 tablespoons water

$1/2$ garlic clove, crushed with a pinch of salt

$1/2$ teaspoon baharat, or ground allspice

1 teaspoon extra virgin olive oil

1 medium bunch (about 30g) of flat-leaf parsley or coriander, leaves picked and roughly chopped

$1/2$ teaspoon dried Turkish (mild) chilli flakes or hot paprika

Boil the pasta in salted water until a little *al dente.* While the pasta is cooking, fry the pine nuts with the butter over a medium heat until the butter and pine nuts are very light brown. Set aside and keep warm. Mix the yoghurt with the garlic and baharat or ground allspice and set aside.

Drain the pasta in a colander and place in a bowl. (If you prefer to eat this dish at room temperature, refresh the pasta with cold water.) Toss the pasta with the olive oil to prevent it from sticking. Mix with the yoghurt and parsley and serve with the warm pine nuts and butter spooned on top and a sprinkling of dried chilli. Eat immediately, as the dish will go stodgy if it sits around.

Pipas – toasted sunflower seeds

If you look on the ground of any Spanish plaza you will notice small piles of sunflower seed husks. Chatting and eating pipas is a great Spanish pastime. It takes a while to master the technique of popping a pipa in your mouth and deftly extracting the kernel without eating any husk.

Per 100 g sunflower seeds, dissolve 2–3 teaspoons of sea salt in 4 teaspoons of water with 1 teaspoon of plain flour. Toss the seeds in the salt and flour solution. Spread thinly on a baking tray, then crisp and dry out for $1^1/_2$–2 hours at 80°C or for 3–4 days in a conservatory, greenhouse or in full sun.

Vegetables

Spring vegetable pilav

Later in the season you can substitute courgettes, runner beans or green tomatoes for the vegetables below – whatever you have ready at the time and need to use up. Follow the method as the basic rule of thumb for making the pilav, but adapt the vegetables according to the season. Delicious on its own with seasoned yoghurt, or with any meat or fish.

Serves 4 as a main course, 6 as a side dish

75g unsalted butter

4cm piece of cinnamon stick

6 allspice berries

1 large or 2 medium onions, thinly sliced

1 large globe artichoke, prepared (see page 55)

1 large bunch of spring onions (about 10–12)

300g basmati rice, soaked in tepid salted water for 1 hour

300g bunch of asparagus, tips kept intact, the tender part of the stem cut in 1cm rounds

80g podded peas

120g podded broad beans (any that are larger than your thumbnail should be blanched for 1 minute and then peeled)

450ml seasoned vegetable, or light chicken stock, hot

a small bunch (about 15g) of dill, chopped

2 tablespoons finely chopped fresh mint

To serve

$^1/_2$ garlic clove, crushed to a paste with a pinch of salt

150g good-quality Greek yoghurt, such as Total, thinned with 4 tablespoons water

Heat the butter in a medium saucepan with the cinnamon and allspice until it foams. Add the onion and a good pinch of salt and cook over a medium heat for 20–25 minutes, until the onion is soft and golden brown. Thinly slice the prepared artichoke heart and cut two-thirds of the spring onions into 2cm lengths; add both to the pot and fry for a few minutes. Drain the rice and add to the pan, stirring for a minute or so to coat it in the butter. Then add the asparagus, peas, broad beans, stock and half the dill. Taste for seasoning – it is best to get the salt right at this stage. Cover with a circle of grease-proof paper and a tight-fitting lid. Bring to the boil, continue to cook over a medium heat for 5 minutes, then reduce the heat to low and cook for a final 5 minutes. Remove from the heat and leave to rest for 5 minutes. Meanwhile, stir the crushed garlic into the Greek yoghurt.

Thinly slice the remaining spring onions and stir them into the rice with the mint and the remaining dill. Taste for seasoning once more and serve with the yoghurt on the side.

Mechouia

Mechouia is like a North African version of the Spanish grilled vegetable salad, escalivada, but with the added intensity and complexity of the spices.

We got the idea of using an old wheelbarrow as a barbecue from a friend, Jane, who invited us to her allotment open day last summer. When we were up on the allotment taking photographs for this book, we spotted an abandoned wheelbarrow with a flat tyre and couldn't resist.

Serves 4

2 large red peppers
3 new season's onions (or 1 red
    onion and a bunch of spring
    onions)
2 medium aubergines
2 courgettes, trimmed, cut into
    long slices 5mm thick

10–12 cherry tomatoes, on the vine
    if possible
a small bunch (about 20g) of
    coriander, leaves picked
$1/2$ teaspoon caraway seeds

Dressing

1 small garlic clove
1 level teaspoon salt
1 teaspoon freshly ground cumin
1 teaspoon freshly ground caraway
juice of 1 lemon

1 tablespoon Harissa (see page 271)
$1/2$ tablespoon good-quality red wine
    vinegar
$1/2$ teaspoon unsmoked paprika
4 tablespoons extra virgin olive oil

We make the dressing in a mortar and pestle, which you can also use for grinding the spices. Pound the garlic with the salt until a smooth paste is formed, then mix in the remaining ingredients. Check the seasoning and set aside.

Preheat a barbecue 20–30 minutes before you want to use it. Grill the peppers, onions and aubergines until soft all the way through and blackened on the outside. The onions will take the longest – about 30–45 minutes until completely soft – the peppers and aubergines only about 15 minutes. If you are without a barbecue, or it is raining, place the whole vegetables under a hot grill or on the naked flame of a gas hob until the skins are charred and crisp, then if necessary finish them off on a roasting tray in an oven preheated to

220°C/425°F/Gas 7, until tender. Grill the courgettes and tomatoes on the barbecue or a griddle pan until lightly charred and tender – they will take less time, about 5–10 minutes.

Remove the vegetables and let them cool a little. Peel the charred skin off the peppers and aubergines and the charred outer layer off the onions. Seed and core the peppers. Tear the flesh of the peppers, aubergines and onions into wide strips and place in a large bowl with the courgettes and tomatoes. Pour over the dressing, add the coriander leaves and season with a little salt and pepper. Toss gently and taste. Scatter with the caraway seeds to finish.

Fried piquillo peppers with thyme

Piquillo peppers are small, firm red peppers from Navarra, which you can find bottled or tinned in many supermarkets and delicatessens. This is a quick side dish that we serve with Venison and crispy potatoes (page 245).

Serves 4

$^1/_2$ teaspoon thyme leaves

$^1/_2$ garlic clove

$^1/_2$ teaspoon sea salt

$^3/_4$ tablespoon good-quality red wine vinegar sweetened with a pinch of sugar

2 tablespoons extra virgin olive oil

8 tinned piquillo peppers, or use 4 red peppers, charred, skinned and seeded

For the dressing crush the thyme and garlic with the salt in a mortar and pestle until smooth. Add the vinegar and olive oil and season with a little black pepper.

Put a large frying pan over a medium to high heat. When hot, lay the peppers in the pan in one layer without adding any oil. When they have a mottled, blackened look on one side, take them out and toss in a bowl with the dressing. Serve warm.

Peas and lentils

The textural combination of peas and lentils is pleasing and the herby dressing gives freshness and life. This versatile dish can accompany most things, yet is particularly good with Tuna with Rosemary Manteca (see page 211).

Serves 4

170g small brown lentils

1 garlic clove, sliced

1 bay leaf

600ml water

250g shelled peas or petits pois, fresh or frozen

1 tablespoon roughly chopped fresh mint

1 tablespoon very finely shredded fresh sage

5 tablespoons extra virgin olive oil

1 tablespoon lemon juice

1 teaspoon sweet red wine vinegar, such as Forum (or use any good-quality red wine vinegar with a pinch of sugar)

Put the lentils, garlic and bay leaf in a medium saucepan and cover with the water. Bring to the boil, then reduce the heat and simmer gently for 15–20 minutes, until the lentils are just tender, topping up the water should it fall below the level of the lentils. They should be cooked but firm and definitely not soft, as it is important that they retain their shape. Remove from the heat, season with salt and set aside.

Half fill another saucepan with salted water and bring to the boil. Add the peas and simmer for about 2 minutes for fresh peas, 30 seconds for frozen ones, until tender. Drain well and transfer to a large bowl. Drain the warm lentils, reserving a little of their liquid. Add them to the bowl of peas with the reserved liquid, the mint, sage, olive oil, lemon juice and vinegar. Season with salt and pepper, stir well and check for seasoning. Serve warm.

Courgettes with almonds

There are many varieties of courgettes you can grow. We particularly like the pale varieties that you find in Greek and Turkish shops, the ridged zucchini from Italy, and the yellow courgettes that make any dish look stunning when mixed with green ones. This dish is good with or without the tomatoes.

Serves 4

1kg courgettes, topped, tailed, and sliced into thin rounds
1 teaspoon fine sea salt
5 tablespoons olive oil
75g whole blanched almonds

2 small garlic cloves, thinly sliced
250g cherry tomatoes, blanched, peeled, halved and seeded (optional)
1 tablespoon roughly chopped fresh mint

Toss the courgettes with the salt and place in a colander. Allow them to sit for at least 10 minutes over a draining board or sink, then pat dry with some kitchen paper.

In a large saucepan, heat the olive oil over a medium heat. Add the almonds and fry for a few minutes, until they just start to turn a pale pink-brown, then remove them with a slotted spoon and add the courgettes to the pan. Cook for about 10 minutes, stirring occasionally, until softened. Add the garlic, tomatoes (if using) and half the mint and continue to cook for about 15 minutes, until very soft, sweet and starting to break down. Now return the almonds to the pan and cook for 5 minutes more, squashing any bits of tomato that are too large for your liking. Add the remaining mint, season with salt and pepper and serve.

Fried marrow with caramelised butter, mint and yoghurt

Whenever the challenge of making something with marrow presents itself, perhaps you, like us, tend to shudder at the thought of stuffed marrow and move on to more accessible vegetables. This year, however, please consider this dish that is delicious with roast chicken or lamb and some simply cooked lentils. It is perfect for that late-summer glut of marrows (or overgrown courgettes) that leaves most of us at a loss what to do with them. If we can find marrows in mid-summer with tender skins, we try to use them. If you can scratch through the skin with your nail, it is tender enough to eat.

Serves 4

1 small, young marrow (about 1kg)
1 teaspoon fine sea salt
75g unsalted butter
$^1/_4$ garlic clove
$^1/_4$ teaspoon cumin seeds, roasted in a dry frying pan

150g good-quality Greek yoghurt, such as Total, thinned with 3–4 tablespoons water
1 tablespoon shredded fresh mint
a pinch of dried Turkish (mild) chilli flakes

Top and tail your marrow and peel it unless the skin is very tender. Cut the marrow in half lengthways and gently scoop out the seeds and the pulpy flesh with a metal spoon. Slice the marrow into half-moon shapes, the width of your index finger, toss them evenly with the salt and put them in a colander. Leave to stand for 10 minutes, then pat dry with kitchen paper.

Heat the butter in a 30cm frying pan over a medium heat until it caramelises, the solids turning light brown. Fry the marrow in 2 batches for 2–3 minutes on each side, until lightly coloured. When the marrow is cooked, it should be soft but not limp.

Crush the garlic and cumin with a pinch of salt until smooth. Stir them into the yoghurt along with half the fresh mint and season with salt and pepper. Serve the hot marrow with the yoghurt spooned on top, scattered with the chilli flakes and remaining mint.

Green beans with tomato and fenugreek sauce

We don't use fenugreek seed very often at Moro, as it only crops up every now and then in Mediterranean cookery. However, when we do, we are always reminded of how interesting it is. If prepared properly, the flavour is subtle and the texture so good.

One of our allotment neighbours makes fantastic use of her green beans. In late spring she plants the seedlings around the perimeter of her fence. As they grow, they slowly form a wall of plants so thick that they entirely enclose the plot, making it completely windproof and private!

Serves 4

400g tender green beans, topped

Tomato and fenugreek sauce

$1^1/_2$ tablespoons fenugreek seeds
6 tablespoons olive oil
2 garlic cloves, thinly sliced
6cm piece of cinnamon stick
800g sweet tomatoes, blanched,
    peeled, seeded and roughly
    chopped

a small bunch (about 20g) of
    coriander, leaves picked
1 tablespoon finely chopped fresh
    red chilli

Bring a large pot of well-salted water to the boil, add the beans and cook for about 5 minutes, until they are tender, not *al dente*. They should just lose their raw vegetable taste and crunch and become slightly sweet. Drain, refresh in cold water, then drain again and set aside.

Place the fenugreek seeds in a small saucepan. Cover generously with cold water, bring to the boil and simmer for a minute. Drain and repeat the process twice, until the fenugreek is tender and tastes inoffensively bitter. Drain and set aside.

Heat the olive oil in a saucepan over a medium to high heat. Add the garlic and cinnamon and fry until the garlic is light brown. Then add the tomatoes and a good pinch of salt to balance their acidity. Cook over a medium heat for about 15–20 minutes, or until the sauce has reduced and thickened. Stir in the fenugreek and the green beans and mix well whilst heating through. Toss with the coriander leaves and red chilli, taste for seasoning once more and serve.

Artichokes and potatoes with oloroso sherry

This dish is delicious on its own or served with fish, meat – pretty much everything!

We grow a variety of potatoes on the allotment, including Yukon Gold, Linzer Delikatess and Pink Fir Apple. Hopefully by the time you read this book, there will be a link showing Sam demonstrating how to prepare artichokes at www.moro.co.uk.

Serves 4

500g small or new potatoes, scrubbed

5 medium globe artichokes

8 tablespoons (120ml) olive oil

1 medium onion, thinly sliced

1 large garlic clove, thinly sliced

150ml medium oloroso sherry

100ml water

$1^1/_2$ tablespoons roughly chopped fresh mint

Cook the potatoes in boiling salted water until tender, then drain. Peel them when they are cool enough to handle, cutting any that are large in half, and set aside.

To prepare the artichokes, see page 55. Cut the prepared hearts into small wedges no more than 1.5cm thick.

Place a large, heavy saucepan over a medium heat and add 6 tablespoons of the olive oil. When it is hot, stir in the onion and a pinch of salt and turn the heat to medium-low. Fry for about 10 minutes, until the onion is soft and starting to colour. Add the artichokes and fry for a further 15 minutes, stirring occasionally, until the onion is golden and the artichokes partly cooked. Now add the garlic, cook for 1 minute more, and pour in the sherry and water. Add half the mint. Put the potatoes on top and cover with a circle of greaseproof paper and a lid. Steam the artichokes and potatoes for about 5 minutes or until the artichokes are tender. Drizzle with the remaining olive oil. The sauce should be quite wet but if not, add an extra splash of water. Check the seasoning and sprinkle on the remaining mint. Serve warm or at room temperature.

Baked beetroot with horseradish and almond sauce

When you bake beetroot whole as you would a potato, the flavour intensifies, accentuating its natural sweetness and earthiness. With the horseradish and almond sauce, this is delicious as a stand-alone dish, although you could also serve it with thinly sliced rare beef or as a salad with broad beans (see page 124). We often roast the beetroot wrapped in foil in the low embers of a barbecue. A couple of years ago we planted some horseradish in the garden, but it takes a long time for the root to thicken – ours is no thicker than a thin carrot, so we have a while to wait yet, which will be too late.

Serves 4

1kg small–medium beetroot, washed
   carefully without piercing the skin

Horseradish and almond sauce

50g whole blanched almonds

40g finely grated fresh horseradish

1 tablespoon sherry vinegar

150ml double cream

1 tablespoon milk

Preheat the oven to 220°C/425°F/Gas 7.

   Wrap the beetroots individually in foil and place directly on the middle shelf of the hot oven. Bake for around $1^1/_2$–$2^1/_2$ hours, until tender (the blade of a sharp knife should slip in easily). Remove from the oven and peel when cool enough to handle. Alternatively, boil the beetroot until tender.

   About half an hour before the beetroot are ready, prepare the sauce. Put the almonds in a food processor and blitz until reasonably fine, leaving a few small chunks for texture. Transfer to a mixing bowl and add the grated horseradish. Stir in the vinegar and season with salt and pepper. Lastly, just before serving, stir in the cream and milk until just mixed. Do not over-mix or the sauce will become solid. Check for seasoning. Serve the beetroot hot or cold with the sauce.

Braised celery with tomato, olives and coriander

The combination of celery and spices seems to work very well, particularly in this recipe, as it transforms the celery into something tasty and exotic.

Serves 4

1 head celery, trimmed and cut into 2cm slices at a very slight angle
5 tablespoons olive oil
2 teaspoons grated garlic
$1/2$ teaspoon fine sea salt
2 tablespoons finely chopped fresh coriander
2 medium tomatoes, blanched, peeled and grated on the coarse blade of a grater

$1/4$ teaspoon ground ginger
$1/4$ teaspoon turmeric
a good pinch of black pepper
$1/2$ teaspoon paprika
10 cracked green olives, rinsed and drained

Fill a medium saucepan with lightly salted water and bring to the boil. Add the celery and blanch for 1 minute, then drain in a colander and set aside. Dry the saucepan, return it to a medium heat and add the olive oil. When it is hot, add the garlic and fry until it just begins to colour, then add the celery and stir once more. Now add the salt, coriander, tomatoes, ginger, turmeric, black pepper and paprika. Stir to mix all the spices with the celery, then cook for 5 minutes. Add the olives and simmer for another 2 minutes, stirring occasionally. Remove from the heat and serve either immediately or at room temperature.

Fried green tomatoes with garlic and sweet vinegar

We eat fried green tomatoes at the beginning of the season to thin out the crop and at the end, when the summer sun has lost its power to ripen. Green tomatoes, unlike red, remain pleasantly crunchy when cooked.

Serves 4

5 tablespoons olive oil

800g green tomatoes, cut into
2–3cm wedges

3 garlic cloves, cut into thin
matchsticks

2 pinches of dried red chilli flakes

1 teaspoon roughly ground cumin

1 tablespoon sweet red wine vinegar
or Pedro Ximénez vinegar (or
balsamic vinegar)

In a wide frying pan (30cm at least, otherwise fry the tomatoes in 2 batches), heat the olive oil over a high heat. When just hot, add the tomatoes, cut-side down, in a single layer, and fry for a few minutes until browned on the first side. Turn over, one by one, to fry the second cut side. As soon as this starts to colour, shuffle the tomatoes around to make a little room for the garlic and one pinch of chilli flakes and the cumin, tucking the garlic in so it makes contact with the pan. Once the garlic is a light nut-brown, season the dish with salt, pepper and the vinegar. Serve immediately or at room temperature, sprinkled with the remaining chilli.

Braised fennel with jamón

Serves 4

5 tablespoons olive oil
4 medium fennel bulbs, trimmed
   and cut into 2cm wedges,
   keeping the green leaves aside
50g jamón, finely chopped into
   matchsticks

1 garlic clove, thinly sliced
75ml water
a squeeze of lemon (optional)
a few extra fennel leaves, chopped,
   if you have them
1 tablespoon chopped fresh mint

Heat the oil in a very wide saucepan over a medium to high heat. When the oil is hot but not smoking, add the fennel and a pinch of salt and cook for 10 minutes, turning the fennel pieces one by one as they colour. Then turn the heat down to medium-low and continue to cook for 15 minutes, stirring from time to time, until the fennel is nicely golden and caramelised all over. Now add two-thirds of the jamón and the garlic and cook for another 5 minutes. Pour in the water, cover the pan and continue cooking for 10 minutes, stirring occasionally, until the fennel is soft and tender, with some of it starting to break up. Add a squeeze of lemon (if using) and the remaining jamón, check for salt and add a few grinds of black pepper. Serve immediately, scattered with the chopped fennel leaves and the mint.

Fried okra with pomegranates and yoghurt

Okra is originally from sub-tropical Africa and its appearance almost seems prehistoric to us. In fact it is part of the mallow family and was first brought to the Mediterranean through Egypt several hundred years ago. It is popular in much of the Eastern Mediterranean today. There is a magic moment worth achieving in cooking okra when it loses its green taste, becomes tender and sumptuous, yet does not break up.

Serves 4

5 tablespoons olive oil

500g small okra, trimmed at the
   top

1 teaspoon coriander seeds

150g good-quality Greek yoghurt,
   such as Total, thinned with 4
   tablespoons milk or water

$^1/_2$ garlic clove, crushed with a
   pinch of salt

seeds of 1 pomegranate

3 tablespoons fresh coriander or
   mint leaves

Put the oil in a wide saucepan over a medium to high heat. When hot, add the okra and the coriander seeds with a pinch of salt. With a lid on, fry for about 10 minutes, stirring or shaking often, until the okra are tender and vivid green, perhaps slightly browned at the edges. Remove to a serving dish. Season the yoghurt with the garlic and spoon it over the okra. Scatter with the pomegranate seeds and the coriander or mint leaves and serve.

Okra and nut pilav

This deliciously textured pilav can accompany almost any simply cooked meat or fish and can be served with either seasoned yoghurt or Tahini Sauce (see page 265).

Serves 4–6

250g okra, sliced in 1cm rounds

3 tablespoons olive oil

75g unsalted butter

1 large or 2 medium onions, finely chopped

1$\frac{1}{2}$ teaspoons fine sea salt

1 teaspoon ground cinnamon

50g shelled unsalted pistachios

50g pine nuts

50g whole blanched almonds

50g walnut halves, broken up slightly

300g basmati rice, soaked in tepid, salted water for 1 hour

450ml vegetable stock (or 450ml boiling water mixed with 2 teaspoons Marigold vegetable bouillon)

a big pinch (about 50 strands) of saffron, soaked in 3 tablespoons boiling water

seeds of 1 pomegranate

a small bunch (about 20g) of coriander, chopped

Sauté the okra in the oil over a high heat, with a pinch of salt, until vivid green and just tender. Remove from the heat and set aside.

Heat the butter in a medium saucepan until it foams, add the onion and salt and cook over a high heat for 2–3 minutes, until just translucent. Add the cinnamon and all the nuts, reduce the heat to medium-low and cook for 20–30 minutes, until the onion is golden and sweet. Drain the rice and add to the pan, stirring it well for a minute or two to coat with the butter, then add the stock and taste for seasoning. Cover the pan with a circle of greaseproof paper and a tight-fitting lid and boil over a medium heat for 5 minutes, then reduce the heat to low and simmer for 5 minutes more.

Remove the greaseproof paper and pour the saffron-infused water over the rice. Spread the okra on top, replace the lid and leave, off the heat, for 10 minutes for the okra to warm through and the rice to rest. To serve, stir half the pomegranate seeds and coriander through the rice and scatter the rest on top.

Hassan's cracked potatoes with coriander

Hassan has the next-door plot to us. He is not only a wonderful gardener but also an excellent cook. Often when you dig up two or three potato plants, there is an annoying amount of undersize potatoes knocking around. Hassan recommends this way of cooking potatoes as a particularly good way of using up the little guys.

As a plant, coriander is an extremely versatile herb – you can eat its roots, leaves and if your plant has gone to seed, as often happens, there is nothing more delicious than biting into a fresh coriander seed. As the seed pops, its aromatic, lemony juices fill your mouth – quite different from the more earthy coriander leaf. Dry coriander seeds, however, are also perfect for this dish.

Serves 6

1kg small waxy or new potatoes, such as Jersey Royal, Charlotte Anya or Ratte, scrubbed, skins on	10 tablespoons (150ml) olive oil
1 heaped teaspoon fine sea salt	1 tablespoon coriander seeds, cracked in a mortar and pestle
	1 glass of red wine

Crack each potato slightly with a heavy object such as a metal cup (opposite), rolling pin or mallet. Toss with the salt and let them stand for 5 minutes. Choose a large saucepan, wide enough to accommodate the potatoes in a single layer (i.e. about 30cm), and place over a medium heat. Add the olive oil and, when it is just hot, the coriander seeds and potatoes. Stir well, cover with a tight-fitting lid and turn the heat to low.

Cook for approximately 20–30 minutes, giving the pan a good shake every 5 minutes, until the potatoes are tender and partly browned (raise the heat towards the end of cooking, if necessary). Pour over the red wine and add a little black pepper, shake well again, then boil, uncovered, for a couple of minutes to get rid of the alcohol. Switch off the heat and let the potatoes sit for 5 minutes.

To serve, scoop up the potatoes with a little of the flavoursome olive oil, red wine and coriander liquor, which you should spoon over them.

Mushroom and potato al forn

During the mushroom season, from late summer until the first frosts of winter, we cook a lot with mushrooms. We ate this particular dish in the foot-hills of the Pyrenees, with some delicious roast lamb. You can use a mixture of wild mushrooms or, if the choice is limited, just oyster mushrooms will do fine.

Serves 4

500g firm potatoes, such as Cyprus, peeled and thinly sliced (no more than 5mm thick)

$^{1}/_{2}$ garlic clove, crushed with a pinch of salt

1 teaspoon fine sea salt

250g mushrooms – oyster, chanterelles, porcini, pieds de mouton – cleaned (and halved if large)

1 scant tablespoon fresh thyme leaves

2 bay leaves, halved lengthways

1 tablespoon finely chopped fresh flat–leaf parsley

5 tablespoons olive oil

4 tablespoons white wine

To serve

1 tablespoon finely chopped fresh flat–leaf parsley

$^{1}/_{2}$ teaspoon smoked sweet paprika

Preheat the oven to 230°C/450°F/Gas 8.

Toss the sliced potatoes with the garlic, salt and some black pepper in a large bowl. Now add the rest of the ingredients and toss again to mix well. Spread the mixture out in a 20 x 30cm roasting tin and cover tightly with foil. Place in the hot oven and roast for 25–30 minutes, until the potatoes are cooked through. Uncover and cook under a hot grill for about 10 minutes to colour the top. Sprinkle with the parsley and paprika before serving.

Fried potatoes with coriander

Lebanese in origin, these potatoes are delicious with fish, chicken, Grilled Poussins with Zaatar (page 251) and Tahini Sauce (page 265). At the restaurant, we use new season's garlic when it arrives at the beginning of April.

Serves 4

1kg smallish firm, waxy potatoes, all roughly the same size, lightly scrubbed

2 garlic cloves, finely chopped

$1/2$ teaspoon ground cumin

10 spring onions, thinly sliced

a large bunch (about 50g) of coriander, chopped, stalks and all (save a few whole leaves to garnish)

8 tablespoons (120ml) olive oil

Put the potatoes in a large pot of cold salted water and bring to the boil. Cook for 15–20 minutes, until just tender, then drain immediately. Peel the potatoes once they are cool enough to handle, then cut in 2cm chunks. Gently toss these with the garlic, cumin, half the spring onions and half the coriander, taking care not to break up the potatoes. Season with salt and pepper.

Heat the olive oil in a very wide non-stick frying pan over a medium-high heat. Add the potatoes and fry gently on one side for about 10 minutes, without moving them around too much, until they are golden with a few crispy bits. Turn them over with a spatula and fry until the other side is also golden and the potatoes tender, scraping up any broken bits of potato from the base of the pan. Toss with the remaining chopped coriander and spring onions and taste for seasoning. Serve with the whole coriander leaves on top.

Crispy potatoes

We use a mandolin to slice these potatoes, as cutting them a uniform size helps them crisp evenly. Conscientious slicing with a sharp knife will do just as well.

Serves 4

1 garlic clove

2 teaspoons finely chopped fresh
   rosemary

1 teaspoon fine sea salt

500g firm, waxy potatoes, peeled

5 tablespoons olive oil

Preheat the oven to 220°C/425°F/Gas 7.

     Crush the garlic, rosemary and salt to a smooth paste in a mortar and pestle. Carefully slice the potatoes lengthways to the thickness of a match. Rub them thoroughly with the garlic paste, then toss with the olive oil and some black pepper. Take a large, non-stick baking tray (if it's not non-stick, line it with a silicone liner), either a round one 40cm in diameter or a 30 x 40cm rectangular one. Arrange the potatoes in a single layer on the tray, over-lapping them slightly, like the scales of a fish. Pour any excess marinade back over the potatoes and roast in the oven for 30–40 minutes, turning the tray occasionally to ensure even cooking. After 15 minutes you might find a few pieces of potatoes are a perfect colour before the rest are golden brown – keep on cooking until the majority have browned. Take out of the oven and eat warm (if you make this in advance, it can be reheated in the oven for a couple of minutes).

Papas aruglas – wrinkled potatoes

These 'wrinkled potatoes' are a speciality of the Canary Islands, partly because of the variety of potato and the volcanic soil they grow in, and partly because of the cooking method. Once ready, they almost look like part of the volcanic soil from which they originate. They are delicious served with Mojo Rojo or Mojo Verde (see pages 268 and 271). At Moro, we serve them with roast pork and Mojo Verde.

Serves 4

1kg small waxy or new potatoes, such as Jersey Royal, Ratte or Anya,
    washed well without breaking the skins

Place the potatoes in a single layer in a wide (25–30cm) saucepan and add
enough cold water to come two-thirds of the way up the potatoes. Make the
water as salty as tears (with 1 tablespoon of salt, or slightly more). Cover with
a lid (leave it open just a crack, so the steam can escape), place over a medium heat and boil for 20–30 minutes, turning down the heat at the end until all
the water has evaporated and the skins of the potatoes have a white, salty
crust and may have started to colour on the bottom. Leave to rest, uncovered,
for 5–10 minutes, as they are too hot to eat immediately, and only take on their
typical wrinkled appearance as they start to cool down.

Pumpkin pisto

Pisto is Spanish ratatouille, of which there are many versions, this one with pumpkin or squash. We make it with a mixture of butternut (a good all-rounder), ironbark and starchy kabocha squash for different flavours and textures. Since we grow a lot of pumpkins of varying varieties on the allotment, we are always looking for new recipes. This one is great with pork, chicken or lamb.

Serves 4

800g peeled and seeded pumpkin or
    squash (roughly 1.2kg weight
    before preparation), cut into
    2cm chunks
$1/2$ teaspoon fine sea salt
6 tablespoons olive oil
$1^1/2$ large or 3 medium onions,
    roughly chopped
1 red pepper, seeded and cut into
    1cm chunks
2 garlic cloves, thinly sliced
4 bay leaves, preferably fresh
$1^1/2$ teaspoons finely chopped fresh
    rosemary

1 tablespoon chopped fresh oregano
    or marjoram
a few grates of nutmeg
$1/2$ teaspoon ground cumin
12 tablespoons (180ml) passata or
    fritada (Spanish tomato sauce)
2 tablespoons sweet red wine
    vinegar, such as Cabernet
    Sauvignon (or use any good-quality
    red wine vinegar and a pinch of
    sugar), mixed with 4 tablespoons
    water
2 tablespoons pine nuts, lightly
    toasted

Toss the pumpkin with the salt and set aside. In a wide saucepan (about 30cm), heat the olive oil over a medium heat, then add the onions with a pinch of salt. Stir well and cook, stirring often, for 15–20 minutes until the onions are soft and beginning to caramelise. Now add the chopped red pepper, fry for a further 10 minutes, then follow with the garlic, bay leaves and rosemary. Continue to cook for a couple of minutes, before adding the pumpkin (blotted dry if wet). Reduce the heat and fry for 20 minutes, until the pumpkin is barely tender, turning it every now and then. Add the oregano or marjoram, nutmeg and cumin, followed by the passata. Cook for 5–10 minutes, until the pumpkin is completely tender, then sprinkle with the vinegar-water, taste and season with salt and pepper if necessary. Serve warm, with the toasted pine nuts on top.

Jewelled pumpkin rice

This pilav is a real winner. For those who need convincing about pumpkin, this is the dish to try.

Serves 4–6

500g peeled and seeded butternut
    squash (the flesh of a 750g
    squash), cut into 1cm dice
1 teaspoon fine sea salt
2 tablespoons olive oil
a big pinch (about 50 strands) of
    saffron
100g unsalted butter
6cm piece of cinnamon stick
4 allspice berries, crushed
1 large or 2 medium onions, thinly
    sliced across the grain

15g dried barberries (or currants)
50g shelled unsalted pistachios
$1/2$ teaspoon ground cardamom
300g basmati rice, soaked in tepid,
    salted water for 1 hour
450ml vegetable stock (or 450ml
    boiling water mixed with 2
    teaspoons vegetable bouillon)
1 quantity Crispy Caramelised
    Onions, to serve (optional – see
    page 67)

Preheat the oven to 230°C/450°F/Gas 8.

Toss the diced butternut squash with half of the salt and the olive oil. Spread it in a single layer in a baking tray and roast for 30 minutes or until tender. Mix the saffron with 3 tablespoons of boiling water and add 25g of the butter, which should melt. Set aside.

Heat the remaining butter in a medium saucepan with the cinnamon and allspice until it foams, then add the onion and the remaining $1/2$ teaspoon of salt. Fry over a medium heat for 10–15 minutes, stirring occasionally until the onion is soft and starting to colour. Add the barberries, pistachios and cardamon and cook for 10 minutes more, until the onion is golden and sweet. Now drain the rice and add to the pan, stirring for a minute or two to coat, then pour in the stock. Taste for seasoning then scatter with the roast squash. Cover with a circle of greaseproof paper and a tight-fitting lid and cook over a high heat for 5 minutes. Reduce the heat to low and simmer for a final 5 minutes. Remove the lid and the greaseproof paper and drizzle with the buttery saffron water. Replace the lid and leave to rest, off the heat, for 5–10 minutes. Serve with a scattering of crispy onions, if you like.

Couscous Royal

This is a perfect way to use up a variety of vegetables you may have either at home or on the allotment. Every now and then at Moro we omit the meat and serve it as a vegetarian main course. We then like to add 20g dried porcini to the broth to give it a little more body, as well as upping the spice by about 50 per cent. This recipe was given to us by Fatima, the wife of our chef Mohammed.

Serves 6–8

100ml olive oil

1kg lamb shanks or neck on the bone (ask the butcher to cut the neck into 2–3cm pieces), or 800g boneless beef shin or chuck, diced

1 onion, thinly sliced across the grain

100g tomatoes, chopped

2 teaspoons finely chopped fresh flat-leaf parsley

a large pinch (about 50 strands) of saffron

$^3/_4$ teaspoon ground ginger

$^3/_4$ teaspoon ground cinnamon

$1^1/_2$ teaspoons turmeric

1 dessertspoon fine sea salt

3 litres water

3kg mixed vegetables: courgettes, turnips (very important), prepared artichoke hearts (see page 55), cabbage, peppers, carrots, peeled and seeded pumpkin etc., all cut into large chunks

Harissa (see page 271), to serve

Onion sauce

500g onions, thinly sliced across the grain

$^1/_2$ teaspoon saffron strands

125g golden sultanas

$^1/_2$ heaped teaspoon turmeric

$^1/_2$ teaspoon ground ginger

$^1/_2$ teaspoon ground cinnamon

4 tablespoons olive oil

200ml water

4 dessertspoons caster sugar

Couscous

800g couscous, preferably fine

50ml olive oil

1 dessertspoon fine sea salt

Put the olive oil in the bottom half of a couscoussier or saucepan steamer big enough to hold the meat and vegetables and place over a medium-high heat. Season the meat with salt and pepper and fry until coloured all over. Now add the onion, chopped tomatoes, parsley, saffron, ginger, cinnamon, turmeric, salt and some black pepper and fry over a low heat for 5–10 minutes, until the onion softens. Add the water, bring to the boil and simmer gently, uncovered, for 1–1$^1/_2$ hours, until the meat begins to soften. Add the vegetables (except the pumpkin) and continue cooking for about 20 minutes.

Meanwhile, make the onion sauce. Put all the ingredients except the water and sugar in a saucepan, add some salt and a good grinding of black pepper and cook over a medium heat for 15–20 minutes, until the onions are soft. Add the water and cook for another 30 minutes, stirring occasionally. Now add the sugar and cook for a further 10 minutes, lid on. Taste and adjust the seasoning if necessary.

To prepare the couscous, place it in a large bowl, cover with cold water and wash. If the couscous is medium, leave in the water for 2 more minutes. Drain in a colander and return to the bowl. Add the olive oil and salt and toss lightly with your hands to mix them in evenly, then set aside until it is dry. Use your fingertips to remove lumps by gently crumbling the couscous until it is light and lump-free. Now is the time to start steaming it in the top half of the couscoussier or steamer. Place a 2cm layer of couscous in the couscoussier and place over the simmering vegetables. Wait a couple of minutes, until the steam rises out from the couscous, then place the remaining couscous on top and steam for about 30 minutes with a lid on.

After the vegetables have been cooking for 20 minutes, add the pumpkin and taste for seasoning. Simmer for 10–15 minutes, until the pumpkin is done and, more importantly, the meat is very tender. Serve the meat and vegetables with plenty of juice, on top of the couscous, with the onion sauce and harissa on the side.

Trinxat

We first ate this dish at a simple restaurant on the outskirts of Barcelona called Can Pineda. It is like a particularly delicious bubble and squeak, and can be eaten either as a starter, a main or as an accompaniment to game, chicken or pork. We have since seen recipes that don't include turnips but we find they lighten the dish and make it more interesting. We often grow turnips on the allotment, not just for the root itself but for their leaves, which are quite wonderful braised with garlic and a little vinegar.

Tocino is the cured back fat of the ibérico (black-foot) pig.

Serves 4

500g firm potatoes, such as Cyprus, peeled and cut into chunks for boiling

6 tablespoons olive oil

8 thin rashers of smoked pancetta or good-quality smoked bacon, rind removed

3 garlic cloves, sliced

60g tocino (Spanish) or lardo (Italian), trimmed and cut into chunky matchsticks (use pancetta if you can't get tocino or lardo)

500g medium turnips, peeled and cut into 1.5cm dice

300g spring greens or Brussels tops, trimmed and cut into bite-sized pieces

1 teaspoon fresh thyme leaves

2 pinches of grated nutmeg (optional and not traditional)

Cook the potatoes in boiling salted water until tender, then drain. Meanwhile, in a large saucepan, heat 2 tablespoons of the olive oil over a medium heat. Add the whole pancetta or bacon rashers and fry for a few minutes, until crisp. Lift them out of the pan and put to one side for later. Add the garlic and tocino pieces to the pan and fry for a couple of minutes, until they begin to colour. Stir in the turnips, cook for 5 minutes, until beginning to soften, then add the greens. Season with salt, pepper and the thyme and nutmeg, if using, and continue to cook for 10 minutes, stirring regularly. If the mixture is starting to catch, turn the heat down low. Remove from the heat and set aside.

Roughly mash the potatoes. Stir them into the turnip mixture and mash a little more. Season with salt and pepper to taste.

Heat another 2 tablespoons of the olive oil in a large frying pan (about 25cm) over a high heat. When hot, tip the turnip mixture into the pan and press down firmly with a spatula or spoon, until the base of the pan is covered. Give the pan a shake, reduce the heat to low and cook for 5 minutes or until brown underneath. To turn over, place a plate on top of the pan and invert the trinxat out on to the plate (this is rather like turning a tortilla – see page 45). Put the last 2 tablespoons of oil into the pan, briefly increase the heat until it starts smoking, then slide the trinxat back in. Again reduce the heat to low and fry for 5 minutes. Serve with the warm, crispy pancetta on top. We would possibly eat this accompanied with a chicory and cos lettuce salad dressed with a sherry or sweet wine vinegar dressing.

Cabbage and bulgur wheat pilav

Our chef, Megan, came up with the idea for this pilav. The combination of the lemony sumac and greens with the bulgur is delicious with fish.

Serves 4

75g unsalted butter

8 spring onions, sliced in 1cm rounds, green and all

50g pine nuts or 80g walnuts

$1/2$ rounded teaspoon ground allspice

600g white cabbage (or spring cabbage or Brussels tops), shredded

200g coarse bulgur, rinsed in cold water and drained

300ml vegetable stock

2 tablespoons sumac (see page 255) (optional)

1 small bunch (about 20g) of parsley, leaves picked and finely chopped

To serve

$1/2$ garlic clove, crushed with a pinch of salt

200g good-quality Greek yoghurt, such as Total

Melt the butter in a saucepan over a medium heat. When it begins to foam, add the spring onions, nuts, allspice and a pinch of salt and cook for 5 minutes. Then stir in the spring greens and after 5 minutes, when they have wilted, the bulgur. Cover with the stock and season with salt and pepper. Lay a circle of greaseproof paper on top and bring to the boil over a medium to high heat. Put a lid on the pan and cook quite fast for 5 minutes. Now turn the heat down to medium-low and cook for another 5 minutes. Stir in the sumac and parsley, switch off the heat and let the pilav sit for 5 minutes.

Stir the garlic into the yoghurt and serve with the pilav.

Fried onions with Malaga wine

Good Malaga wine is one to be reckoned with. Famously made with the muscatel grapes that grow north of the city, it is a sweet wine of the highest quality. This dish is delicious with lamb, pork or chicken. You could use chicory instead of onions, or shallots instead.

Serves 4

40g unsalted butter

2 tablespoons olive oil

300g baby onions or whole
    shallots, or 3 heads of chicory,
    cut into quarters lengthways

75ml Malaga wine, Moscatel
    or sweet oloroso sherry

a few flat-leaf parsley leaves

Place a large frying pan over a medium-high heat and add the butter and olive oil. When the butter begins to foam, add the onions or shallots, or the chicory. Season with salt and pepper and fry for 15–20 minutes, until caramelised and light brown on both sides and tender in the centre. Add the wine or sherry and simmer for a minute or so to burn off the alcohol. Taste for seasoning, adding a splash of water if the sauce is too thick, and dot with the whole parsley leaves.

Fried spiced cauliflower

This is delicious, easy and versatile. It goes with almost any Moorish meat or fish dish accompanied by lentils dressed with olive oil and lemon. A fantastic, less traditional way of using cauliflower.

Serves 4

1 teaspoon coriander seeds

$^1/_2$ teaspoon cumin seeds

$^1/_4$ teaspoon fennel seeds

8 peppercorns

sunflower or olive oil for frying

1 medium head of cauliflower, stalk removed, broken into florets

Maldon sea salt

lemon wedges, to serve

Grind the coriander, cumin and fennel seeds with the peppercorns in a mortar and pestle, then set aside.

Pour 1cm depth of oil into a large saucepan over a medium to high heat. When hot, add the cauliflower and fry on all sides until tender and slightly golden – beware, as the oil is likely to spit (half-cover the pan with a lid if it gets bad). Drain well on kitchen paper and season to taste with Maldon salt.

Mix the spices with a little salt and scatter half the mixture over the cauliflower. Serve with lemon wedges on the side, and the remaining spices in a small bowl for people to dunk their florets in, should they so wish.

Lentil and angel-hair pilav

One could write an unfashionable book of joyous recipes that combine different carbohydrates and this would be one of its stars. This rich and robust pilav from the Lebanon goes well with lamb or chicken, along with a crunchy salad such as beetroot or radish (see pages 124 and 128) and like all our pilavs, yoghurt seasoned with garlic (page 158).

Serves 4

150g brown or green lentils

2 tablespoons olive oil

150g angel-hair pasta (vermicelli/ capelli d'angelo)

50g unsalted butter

1 medium onion, finely chopped

$^1/_2$ rounded teaspoon ground allspice

$^1/_2$ rounded teaspoon ground cinnamon

$^1/_2$ teaspoon freshly ground black pepper

400ml chicken (or vegetable) stock

To serve

1 quantity of Crispy Caramelised Onions (page 67)

sliced raw tomatoes, or Beetroot and Broad Bean Salad (page 124), or Radish, Kohlrabi and Mooli Salad (page 128)

Put the lentils in a medium saucepan and cover with water. Bring to the boil, then reduce the heat and simmer gently for 15–20 minutes, until the lentils are just tender, topping up the water if it falls below the level of the lentils. They should be cooked but firm and definitely not soft, as it is important that they retain their shape. Remove from the heat, season with salt and set aside.

Heat the oil in a medium saucepan. Crush the pasta into the pan with your hands and fry the broken pieces over a medium heat, stirring continuously until they are golden brown. Remove with a slotted spoon and set aside, then add the butter and onion to the pan. Cook for 15–20 minutes, stirring occasionally until the onion is golden and sweet, then add the spices and fry for a few minutes more. Return the pasta to the pan, along with the drained lentils, then add the stock and season with salt to taste. Cover the pan with a circle of greaseproof paper and a tight-fitting lid. Let the mixture boil for 5 minutes, then reduce to a simmer and cook for 5 minutes more. Remove from the heat and leave to rest for 5 minutes. Serve with the crispy onions on top.

Fish Main Courses

Scallops with oloroso sherry, asparagus and migas

Scallops are sweet in flavour, and a sauce made with a nutty, medium oloroso sherry is a perfect partner for them, although a dry sherry such as fino or manzanilla would work well too. If you can't get scallops, then prawns or langoustines make a good alternative.

At Moro we serve this dish with asparagus and crispy saffron migas (fried bread) but a simpler accompaniment would be braised spinach.

Serves 4

5 tablespoons olive oil
$1/2$ large onion, finely chopped
12 large scallops with corals, out of their shell, washed, trimmed of the tough side muscle and patted dry

150ml medium-dry oloroso sherry
a splash of water (about 25ml)

Asparagus
1kg firm green asparagus, medium or thin thickness cut into 4–5cm lengths

2 tablespoons lemon juice
3 tablespoons extra virgin olive oil

Migas
6 tablespoons olive oil
10 garlic cloves, skins on
200g day-old, slightly dry, rustic white bread, such as ciabatta or sourdough, crusts removed, torn into 2cm pieces

2 bay leaves
a good pinch (about 40 strands) of saffron, infused in $3^1/_2$ tablespoons boiling water

To serve
1 tablespoon chopped fresh oregano

1 teaspoon sweet paprika, smoked or unsmoked

Place a small saucepan over a medium heat and add 3 tablespoons of the olive oil. When hot, stir in the onion and a small pinch of salt and fry for about 15–20 minutes, stirring occasionally, until golden brown, caramelised and sweet in flavour. If the onion is colouring too quickly, turn down the heat. Drain off any excess oil and set aside. (This can be done in advance.)

The ends of asparagus can be woody. Gently flex the very end of each spear until the stem snaps off at its natural break. Rinse and drain. Set a large pot of salted water on to boil while you prepare the rest of the ingredients.

For the migas, heat the olive oil in a wide frying pan or saucepan over a low–medium heat. Add the garlic cloves and fry for a few minutes to release their flavour. Turn down the heat further if the garlic is sizzling too quickly, as it is very important that it does not burn. Now add the bread and bay leaves and fry gently for 20–25 minutes, turning and stirring often, until the bread and garlic are golden all over. Pour over the saffron water and continue to cook for 5–10 minutes, until the bread is crunchy again. Remove from the heat, season with salt and keep warm.

Just before you cook the scallops, blanch the asparagus in the pan of boiling salted water for a few minutes, until tender and no longer crunchy. Drain carefully, then dress with the lemon and oil and season with salt and pepper. Keep warm while you quickly finish the scallops.

Set a frying pan over a high heat and add the remaining 2 tablespoons of olive oil. When it is hot add the scallops, seasoned with a little salt and pepper. Sear the scallops for 1–2 minutes on each side, until just golden brown. Then add the softened onion, oloroso and water, taking care it does not spit too much, and gently simmer for another minute.

To serve, spread the dressed warm asparagus out on 4 serving plates. Dot the scallops intermittently between the asparagus spears, followed by the crisp migas, soft garlic and oloroso sauce. Finish with the oregano on top and a generous sprinkling of paprika. Eat immediately.

Tuna with rosemary manteca

We had this dish in Sanlúcar de Barrameda, near Jerez on the Atlantic coast of Andalucía. The idea is similar to putting garlic and parsley butter on a delicious piece of fish but, being Spanish, they use manteca (lard) or jamón fat instead of butter. It is always worth asking in a deli if they have any spare fat from a prosciutto or jamón, as there is often wastage when the ham is trimmed for slicing. You need pure, ivory-white fat, as the yellower fat from the outside of the leg can taste a little rancid, but it doesn't matter if there are tiny flecks of cured ham in the white fat. Alternatively use lardo, which you can find in most Italian delicatessens.

You could substitute any firm white fish for the tuna, such as turbot, monkfish or halibut. We like to serve this dish with Peas and Lentils (see page 163).

Serves 4

100g manteca, jamón fat or lardo, finely chopped	4 tuna steaks (or halibut, turbot or monkfish fillets), about 200g each
1 small garlic clove	2 tablespoons olive oil
$1/2$ heaped tablespoon fresh rosemary	1 lemon, cut into quarters, to serve

Put the chopped fat in a small saucepan and place over a very low heat to melt; this should take 5–10 minutes. Remove from the heat and strain into a bowl, discarding the solids. Let it cool slightly, then place in the fridge to set for an hour or so. Once it is set, chop the garlic and rosemary together until very fine and stir them into the fat. Season with salt and pepper to taste.

Preheat a griddle pan or barbecue to a high heat for tuna, medium-high for other fish. Season the fish with salt and pepper and brush with the oil. Carefully place the tuna on the griddle or barbecue (if you are using another fish with the skin on, place the fillets skin-side down first). Sear for about a minute on each side – serve tuna medium-rare (pink) in the middle, or rarer if you prefer. White fish will take rather longer (several minutes on either side), as it should be cooked through. Remove from the heat and transfer to 4 warm plates. Dab the manteca over the fish, spreading it out with the back of a spoon, and serve with warm lentils and peas and the lemon wedges.

Fish stew with yoghurt and vine leaves

At the end of spring/beginning of summer, vine leaves need pruning. The allotment is full of vines – as hedging for boundaries, above tables as shade from the sun, or simply grown for fruit. Around June it is not uncommon to see our fellow allotment holders trimming the young leaves to turn them into delicious tiny Dolmas (stuffed vine leaves – page 39). At Moro we use the leaves for wrapping mackerel (page 232), sardines, or breast of quail or partridge for roasting. We also like to make this fish stew. The tender leaves are rolled into cigars, sliced thinly and added to the stew like spinach. If you can't get tender young vine leaves for this dish, substitute sorrel. The shop-bought vine leaves in brine are just too tough for this delicate stew.

Serves 4

100g small, fresh vine leaves

2 medium red mullet or 1 sea bream, scaled and gutted

1 small onion, halved

1 large bunch (about 40g) of flat-leaf parsley

700ml water

6 tablespoons olive oil

3 celery sticks, diced small

1 very large fennel bulb (strip the outer layer off with a potato peeler if blemished), diced small

3 garlic cloves, thinly sliced

1 teaspoon whole fennel seeds

3 tablespoons raki (or arak, ouzo or pastis)

4 thin slices of lemon

4 large langoustines or 8 tiger prawns

20 mussels (about 300g), cleaned and de-bearded

400g tin of cannellini beans (or 240g drained cooked cannellini beans), drained and rinsed

150g good-quality Greek yoghurt, such as Total

1 egg yolk

To serve

75g unsalted Caramelised Butter, (see page 6)

$1/_2$ teaspoon dried Turkish (mild) chilli flakes

Pinch the stalks out of the vine leaves and blanch the leaves in a large pan of lightly salted boiling water for 1–2 minutes. Drain and refresh in cold water. Roll the leaves up tightly and shred them thinly with a sharp knife. If using sorrel, there is no need to blanch it; simply shred it and add at the end of cooking.

Cut the mullet or bream into thin steaks (about 1.5cm) and set aside. Use the heads, along with the onion, the stalks from the bunch of parsley, any fennel trimmings and the water to make a light fish stock – just simmer for 10 minutes, then strain and set aside.

Heat the oil over a low heat in a large saucepan and gently fry the celery, fennel, garlic and fennel seeds with a pinch of salt for about 15 minutes, until just tender but not coloured. Now add the finely shredded vine leaves and fry for 2 minutes more.

Measure out 500ml of your fish stock and add it to the pan, along with the raki. Simmer for 3 minutes, then taste the broth for seasoning. Now, all at the same time, add the lemon slices, langoustines or prawns, mussels, fish steaks and beans and stir once (be careful not to break the fish up). Cook with a lid on for 5 minutes, until all the seafood is just done.

Chop the parsley leaves and stir them into the yoghurt, along with the egg yolk. Once the fish is cooked and the mussels open, add a little of the hot broth to the yoghurt, then gently stir it back into the stew. Heat gently until slightly thickened, but don't let it boil. Serve immediately with the caramelised butter drizzled over and the Turkish chilli scattered on top.

Tuna with red onion, tomato and sweet vinegar

On the 'hots' section of the restaurant, this is probably the chefs' most popular dish to cook. The onions should not be too soft or have lost too much colour, the tuna should be cooked to perfection, and the tomatoes heated just long enough to release a little of their juices without turning to a mush. A good splash of vinegar lifts the whole plate, yet without being dominant. The end result is almost like a warm salad.

Serves 4

6 tablespoons olive oil

2 garlic cloves, cut into fine matchsticks

3 red onions (about 400g), sliced Chinese style (see page 243)

4 fresh bay leaves

600g skinless fresh tuna loin or monkfish cut in 3cm cubes

2 teaspoons chopped fresh oregano

350g cherry tomatoes, blanched, peeled, quartered and seeded

300g drained cooked judion beans (150g dry weight), or use cooked butter beans or cannellini beans

1 tablespoon sweet red wine vinegar, like Forum Cabernet Sauvignon (or any good-quality red wine vinegar with a pinch of sugar)

Heat 4 tablespoons of the oil in a medium saucepan over a low heat and fry the garlic in this until crisp and golden brown (take care not to let it burn). Remove the garlic with a slotted spoon and set aside for later. Add the onions and bay leaves to the still-hot pan with a good pinch of salt and increase the heat to medium. Cook for 15 minutes, stirring often, until the onions are softened and beginning to brown. Set aside.

Minutes before you are ready to serve, place a very wide pan over a high heat until smoking. Season the tuna with salt and pepper. Add the remaining 2 tablespoons of oil to the pan and sear the tuna briskly on 2 sides – they will only need about a minute per side. Add the cooked onions, half the oregano, the tomatoes, the beans and the vinegar and sauté for a minute more, until everything is warmed through (the tuna should be quite pink in the middle). Transfer to a serving dish, sprinkle over the remaining oregano and the crispy garlic and serve immediately.

Sea bass with salmorejo and fried aubergines

Salmorejo is a thick tomato gazpacho from the Cordoban region of Andalucía, sometimes served as a sauce to go with fish (or chicken), or as a tapa with fried aubergines. We combine all three for a delicious main course. Enjoy the taste of summer!

Serves 4

2 medium aubergines, halved lengthways and sliced in half-moons 5mm thick
sunflower oil for frying

4 sea bass fillets, about 200g each (grey mullet or sea bream fillets, or hake steaks, are good substitutes)
3 tablespoons olive oil

To serve

1 quantity of Salmorejo Sauce (see page 262)

1 lemon, cut into quarters

First prepare the salmorejo sauce and chill.

Sprinkle the aubergines with fine sea salt and leave for 5 minutes, then pat them dry with kitchen paper. Heat 1cm depth of sunflower oil in a large frying pan or saucepan until hot but not smoking. Fry the aubergines in 2–3 batches, depending on the size of your pan, making sure there are not too many or they will not colour evenly. When golden brown on both sides, remove with tongs or a slotted spoon and drain on kitchen paper. Keep warm in a low oven whilst you fry the remaining aubergines and fish (it is best to cook the fish and aubergines at the same time, so they are ready to serve together).

For the fish, heat a frying pan over a high heat until smoking-hot. Season the sea bass with salt and a little black pepper, drizzle the olive oil into the pan to cover the bottom and gently ease in each fillet, skin-side down, shaking the pan as you go to prevent sticking. Lower the heat to medium and fry the fillets for about 3–4 minutes, depending on thickness, until cooked halfway through. Turn them gently and fry for a couple of minutes more or until just cooked through.

Serve on individual plates with the salmorejo spooned next to the fish and a mound of aubergine slices and a wedge of lemon on each.

Fatima's sardine tagine

Fatima is the wife of our wonderful chef, Mohammed. When we quiz Mohammed about certain Moroccan dishes he says, 'Oh you'll have to ask my wife.' We asked her about this one and discovered that she cooks the sardines for the same amount of time as she cooks the potatoes and that is what makes it taste so deliciously authentic.

Serves 4

8 large, fresh sardines

1 quantity of Charmoula (see page 273)

400g tomatoes, sliced in thin rounds

400g firm, potatoes, peeled, sliced in 5mm rounds and tossed in 1 teaspoon fine sea salt

1 medium green chilli

4 slices of lemon

2 tablespoons olive oil (no more than 5mm)

Scale and gut the sardines (see page 226), then simply fillet them – or ask your fishmonger to do this for you. Lay 8 of the filleted sardines out, skin-side down, and spread half the charmoula over the flesh side. Lay the other 8 fillets on top, skin-side up, to sandwich the charmoula between the fish.

For the tagine, cover the base of a 30cm-wide tagine dish or frying pan with half the tomatoes, followed by the potatoes in a single layer only. Cover the potatoes with the remaining tomatoes, then nestle the sardines on top, placing your chilli in the centre. Dilute the remaining charmoula with 2 tablespoons water and the olive oil and drizzle over the dish. Place a slice of lemon on each pair of fillets and sprinkle with salt and pepper.

Traditionally cooked over coals, this dish can also be cooked over a low barbecue or a medium-low heat on the hob. In either case, cover with a tight-fitting lid for 20–25 minutes, then uncover and cook for another 5–10 minutes, until the potatoes are tender and the sauce thickened.

Halibut with prawn and saffron rice

A delicious concentration of rich Spanish flavours, made by simmering the prawn shells in the stock. This is a good summer rice dish to have in your repertoire. We use halibut or any white fish, depending on what the fisherman has caught overnight.

Serves 4–6

4–6 halibut fillets, 150–200g each, skin on (turbot, monkfish or other firm white fish will be just as good)

3 tablespoons olive oil

Prawn and saffron rice

250g cooked shell-on Atlantic prawns, peeled (reserve the shells)

750ml delicate fish stock

1 large pinch (about 50 strands) of saffron

8 tablespoons (120ml) olive oil

1 medium onion, finely chopped

1 small green pepper, finely chopped

1 small fennel bulb, finely chopped

2 bay leaves

2 garlic cloves, sliced

$1/4$ teaspoon fennel seeds

150g cherry tomatoes, blanched and peeled

200g Calasparra (paella) rice

75ml white wine

To serve

1 lemon, cut into quarters

150g watercress, dressed lightly with olive oil and lemon

1 quantity of Alioli (see page 274), with or without the almonds

Simmer the prawn shells in the fish stock for 5 minutes, then strain through a fine sieve. Measure out 650ml of this broth, discarding any excess. Add the saffron to the stock while it is still hot, to steep.

Heat the 8 tablespoons of olive oil in a paella pan or a large (30cm) frying pan over a medium heat, then add the onion, green pepper, fennel and a good pinch of salt. Fry for 15–20 minutes, until softened and golden, then add the bay leaves, garlic and fennel seeds. Continue cooking for 2 minutes, then add the tomatoes and cook for a further 10 minutes, until they soften, smashing them with the back of a spoon. Now add the rice, stir it around for a couple of minutes to coat, and pour in the wine. Let it bubble for a couple of minutes to evaporate the alcohol. Add the prawn stock, bring to a simmer and taste for seasoning, then reduce the heat to low (it is best to use your largest hob so it cooks evenly). Let it bubble gently until the rice is just a little hard in the middle and still a little wet. Remove from the heat and scatter the peeled prawns on top, then cover with foil and set aside to rest while you cook the fish.

Heat a large frying pan over a high heat until smoking hot. Season the halibut with salt and a little black pepper. Drizzle the olive oil into the pan to cover the bottom and gently ease in each fillet, skin-side down, shaking the pan as you go to prevent sticking. Lower the heat to medium and fry the fillets for 5–8 minutes, depending on thickness. Turn them gently, and fry for a couple more minutes on the second side, until just cooked through. Serve immediately, with the saffron rice on the side, a wedge of lemon, a little alioli and the watercress.

Whole baked sea bass with fennel

A whole baked fish is perfect for a dinner or lunch party, hot or at room temperature. When fennel is at its peak, this is a great way to cook with this delicious vegetable.

Serves 4

1 large sea bass (about 1.5kg), scaled and gutted
$1^1/_2$ teaspoons Maldon sea salt
$^1/_2$ teaspoon coarsely ground black pepper
4 flat-leaf parsley stems
2 medium fennel bulbs, stalks removed and reserved, bulb sliced into wedges 5mm thick

4 thin lemon slices
1 teaspoon fennel seeds
2 bay leaves
1 red onion, thinly sliced
6 tablespoons extra virgin olive oil
6 tablespoons white wine

Preheat the oven to 230°C/450°F/Gas 8.

Rinse the fish inside and out, pat dry, then season inside and out with the Maldon salt and black pepper. Stuff the cavity with the parsley stems, fennel stalks, lemon slices, fennel seeds and bay leaves.

Toss the sliced fennel bulb and red onion with 4 tablespoons of the olive oil, the white wine and a little salt and pepper. Spread the sliced vegetables in a thin layer over the base of a large baking tray, then place the fish on top. Drizzle the fish with the remaining oil and roast in the oven for 35–40 minutes, until just cooked through. Remove from the oven and leave to rest for 5 minutes before serving, either in the roasting tray or in a serving dish with the fennel on the side.

Charcoal grilled sardines with migas

This dish was first prepared for us by Amalia, at the Hotel Berchules in the Alpujarras, in the foothills of the Sierra Nevada. The grilled sardines are served alongside semolina migas, a dish typical of the Granada province of Andalucía. They have an uncanny resemblance to couscous – not altogether surprising, since the Moors lived in the Alpujarras for a hundred years after being banished from Granada. Migas are often served with morcilla (the Spanish equivalent of black pudding), panceta (similar to Italian pancetta), longaniza (a long, thin fresh chorizo sausage), or arenche (salted sprats, similar to anchovies). In leaner times, when there was no meat or fish, the migas would be served with a fried or grilled onion.

Amalia also made Ensalada Piperada, a refreshing chopped salad that is perfect with the crumbly migas. To finish, grapes or pomegranate seeds are scattered on top, a welcome change from lemon wedges.

Serves 4

12 fresh smallish sardines (or 4 mackerel)

Migas

$3^1/_2$ tablespoons olive oil

2 garlic cloves, roughly chopped

250g semolina (or polenta)

450ml tepid water

To serve

Ensalada Piperada (see page 137), made without the avocado

1 bunch of green grapes, such as muscat, and/or the seeds of $^1/_2$ large pomegranate

To make the migas, put the olive oil in a large frying pan or saucepan over a medium heat. When hot, add the garlic, then after 20 seconds add a table-spoon of the semolina and stir until the garlic just begins to turn golden. Adding 1 tablespoon of the semolina early gives a good flavour. Now pour on the water, add salt to taste and bring to the boil. Pour in the rest of the semolina, stirring all the while. As the semolina cooks, it absorbs the water and forms a lumpy mass. Keep stirring and chopping continuously with a metal spatula or spoon until you are left with a more crumb-like texture, with a few little lumps in it. This takes time (about 15–20 minutes) and a strong arm, but is well worth it.

Scaling sardines is easy: just hold each fish under running water and rub from tail to head, as you would a bar of soap. The scales will fall away and any left behind will be easily visible. To gut the fish, make a slit up the length of the belly with a sharp knife under running water and pull out the guts and gills by hand, then cut off the fins with scissors (a fishmonger could easily do all of this for you in a couple of minutes). Pat the sardines dry with kitchen paper. In a large bowl, toss them with a generous quantity of salt, then cover and chill for about half an hour.

If you are grilling over charcoal, light it 20–30 minutes before you wish to cook. If you are grilling under a domestic grill, turn it to a high heat 5 minutes before you are ready; or use a ridged grill pan and preheat it. Grill the sardines for about 2–3 minutes on either side, until the skin is slightly charred and the flesh cooked through to the bone but still juicy. Lay them on a large plate and serve with the migas, ensalada piperada and grapes or pomegranate seeds.

Sea bass with Seville orange sauce

This is a butter sauce, intensely flavoured with Seville oranges, which we find goes very well with fish, braised spinach or chard and boiled potatoes. If you cannot obtain Seville oranges, the sour flavour of their juice can be imitated with a 50:50 mixture of lemon and orange juice.

Serves 4

4 sea bass fillets, about 200g each (grey mullet or bream fillets, or hake steaks, are good substitutes)

3 tablespoons olive oil

Seville orange sauce

100ml Seville orange juice (3–4 oranges) – or use a 50:50 mixture of ordinary orange and lemon juice

1 heaped teaspoon grated Seville (or ordinary) orange zest, briefly blanched in boiling water to remove any bitterness

2 fresh bay leaves

a sprig of thyme

a pinch of ground cinnamon

150g good-quality unsalted butter, cut into cubes

2 teaspoons caster sugar

To make the sauce, place the orange juice and zest, bay, thyme and cinnamon in a small saucepan and bring to a simmer. Stirring constantly with a balloon whisk, add the butter in 3 lots. Keep the pan over a very low heat and make sure that the sauce emulsifies nicely. Strain through a fine sieve into a bowl, add the sugar (to taste) and season with salt. It will take more salt than you might think to balance the acidity. Keep the sauce warm, stirring occasionally, while you cook the fish. You could leave the sauce in a bain-marie, but do not allow it to boil.

Heat a frying pan over a high heat until smoking-hot. Season the sea bass with salt and a little black pepper, drizzle the olive oil into the pan to cover the base and gently ease in each fillet, skin-side down, shaking the pan as you go to prevent sticking. Lower the heat to medium and fry the fillets for 4–5 minutes, until cooked halfway through. Turn them gently and fry for a couple more minutes, until just cooked through. Remove and serve immediately, with the warm sauce spooned over the fish.

Monkfish with sweet onions, ginger, and saffron

When it comes to Mediterranean cooking, it is impossible to get more exotic flavours than in this tagine. Shut your eyes, taste and be transported to Morocco.

Serves 4

1 large monkfish tail, or the thick
    ends of 2 medium ones (about
    1kg in total), on the bone (or use
    4 portion-sized steaks or fillets
    of any firm white fish)
8 tablespoons (120ml) olive oil
2 medium onions, very thinly sliced
    across the grain
2 garlic cloves, thinly sliced
120g golden sultanas

1 teaspoon ground ginger
a medium pinch (about 30 strands)
    of saffron
$1^1/_2$ teaspoons ground turmeric
$1^1/_2$ teaspoons ground cinnamon
400ml water
400g firm potatoes, peeled and cut
    into 2cm dice
1 teaspoon orange blossom water
    (optional)

Even if your fishmonger has skinned the monkfish tail for you, it will probably still need a little trimming and tidying up. Using a very sharp knife, trim off all the external membrane (a thin, pinkish or greyish layer covering the fish), taking care not to lose too much of the flesh as you go. You should end up with 2 pearly white loins of monkfish, joined by the bone in the middle. Set aside while you make the sauce.

Heat 6 tablespoons of the olive oil in a medium saucepan over a medium heat. Add the onions and a pinch of salt and cook for about 10-15 minutes, stirring often, until the onions are soft, sweet and just golden. Now add the garlic and sultanas and fry for 5 minutes more, until the sultanas swell, and perhaps a few of them have caramelised slightly. Stir in all the spices and fry for 1 minute, then pour in the water. Let it simmer for 5 minutes, then remove from the heat. Up to this point, all can be done in advance.

Preheat the oven to 230°C/450°F/Gas 8.

Season the fish with salt and pepper, rub with the remaining 2 tablespoons of olive oil and set aside. Toss the potatoes with a good pinch of salt and leave for a couple of minutes, then stir them into the sauce. Pour the whole lot into a roasting tin large enough to accommodate the fish, cover with foil and put in the oven. The fish must be added at the right point so it will be ready at the same time as the potatoes, which will take 30 minutes once they come to a simmer:

- a large (1kg) monkfish tail will also take 30 minutes or so, and should be added as soon as the potatoes are hot
- 2 smaller tails will take about 20 minutes, so let the potatoes bubble for 10 minutes before adding them
- portion-sized fillets or steaks will take only 10–15 minutes, so let the potatoes bubble for a good 15 minutes before adding the fish.

Once you have added the fish, bake, covered, for half its cooking time. Now turn the fish over, so it gets coated in the sauce, and continue to bake, uncovered, until done. Sprinkle with the orange blossom water, if using, and serve, either with couscous or a green salad.

Grilled mackerel in vine leaves

In Istanbul, different restaurants, whether on the banks of the Bosphorus, the Black Sea or on the Mediterranean, all serve variations of this dish as grilled mackerel with bread and salad is so popular. Sometimes at Moro, we serve it on flatbread to tempt people to eat it like a kebab: the fish (filleted), the cabbage, walnut tarator and pickled chillies all wrapped in bread. Not haute cuisine, perhaps, but it certainly hits the spot.

Serves 4

4 large mackerel or red mullet,
   scaled and gutted
8–12 fresh or bottled vine leaves,
   blanched if fresh, rinsed if bottled

2 tablespoons olive oil
1 quantity of Walnut Tarator
   (page 266)

Cabbage salad

$^1/_2$ large white cabbage (about 500g)
2 teaspoons dried Turkish (mild)
   chilli flakes
50g broken-up shelled walnuts

1 medium bunch (about 20g) of dill,
   coarsely chopped
3 tablespoons extra virgin olive oil
juice of 1 lemon

Preheat a griddle or barbecue.

To prepare the mackerel or mullet, season the fish with sea salt and black pepper, then wrap each one in 2–3 vine leaves. Brush the outside with the olive oil.

For the salad, shred the cabbage as finely as possible. Toss with the chilli flakes, walnuts and dill. Prepare a dressing with the olive oil, lemon juice, salt and pepper and set aside. Do not dress the salad until you are ready to serve.

Briskly grill the fish on the preheated ridged griddle pan or barbecue for 4–5 minutes per side, or until just cooked through. Serve with the dressed salad and tarator sauce.

Meat Main Courses

Kebabs

Much cooking on the allotment happens over charcoal, and each plot holder owns at least one brazier. For this reason, a lot of meat ends up as kebabs, accompanied by fresh salads, grilled peppers or chillies, and herbs, all picked from their patches, as well as yoghurt and flatbread. When we arrived at the allotment we were bowled over by the food – it was so Moro!

We like to serve grilled green chillies, flatbread, yoghurt and herbs with our kebabs, or Tahini Sauce (see page 265) and Chopped Green Salad (page 124). We either make chunky shish kebabs with a variety of marinades (see pages 236-7), or köfte (see below).

Serves 4-6

Köfte

750g minced lamb	1 teaspoon unsmoked sweet paprika
5 tablespoons very finely chopped onion	$^1/_2$-1 teaspoon dried Turkish (mild) chilli flakes (optional)
2 tablespoons finely diced fresh chilli (red or green)	1 teaspoon ground cumin
2 garlic cloves, crushed to a paste with $1^1/_2$ teaspoons fine sea salt	1 medium bunch (about 30g) of coriander, roughly chopped
	freshly ground black pepper

Mix all the ingredients and knead by hand until they begin to bind together. To make köfte, divide the mixture into 8 and work each part into a sausage around a flat skewer, squeezing well to ensure the meat stays on.

To make shish kebabs, dice a skinned, trimmed 1.5kg leg of lamb into 3cm cubes, marinate them as on pages 236-7, then thread 6-7 cubes of meat on to each skewer.

Cooking kebabs

For either köfte or shish, season the outside of the kebabs with salt and pepper. Grill them over quite a high heat (there is no substitute for a charcoal grill) and serve immediately. There is almost no point making a delicious kebab unless you make delicious things to go with it. Be sure to grill a few peppers, make flat bread or buy fine Turkish bread or pitta, and certainly have some yoghurt at the ready, seasoned with a little garlic and salt – it makes all the difference.

Marinades

Below are various marinades to encourage you to try your own. The combination of a delicious marinade and cooking over charcoal gives the meat a wonderful flavour, which cannot be imitated by gas or electric cookers.

Each marinade is sufficient for one of the following: a large chicken, 4 poussins, 8 quail, a 1.5kg boned leg of lamb (or 800–900g trimmed lean leg or shoulder of lamb for kebabs), 12–16 chops, 1kg boneless beef, veal, pork, venison, chicken or lamb as steaks and kebabs, or 4 portions of fish.

Serves 4–6

Yoghurt marinade for chicken, lamb or fish

2 garlic cloves, crushed

juice of $^1/_2$ lemon

1 teaspoon sweet paprika

2 teaspoons cumin seeds, roughly ground

2 teaspoons coriander seeds, roughly ground

a good pinch (about 40 strands) of saffron, soaked in 2 tablespoons boiling water

3 tablespoons roughly chopped fresh coriander

150g good-quality Greek yoghurt, such as Total

2 tablespoons finely grated onion

3 tablespoons olive oil

freshly ground black pepper

Moro classic lamb and chicken marinade

3 garlic cloves, crushed with 1 teaspoon salt

juice of $^1/_2$ lemon

1 level teaspoon hot smoked paprika

1 level teaspoon sweet smoked paprika

2 teaspoons ground cumin

3 tablespoons olive oil

ground black pepper

Pomegranate molasses marinade for chicken, quail, pigeon, pheasant or partridge (whole birds or breasts)

1 garlic clove, crushed

juice of 1 pomegranate (see page 52)

1 teaspoons freshly ground cinnamon

1 tablespoon pomegranate molasses

1 tablespoon finely grated onion

2 tablespoons olive oil

freshly ground black pepper

Pinchitos marinade for veal, chicken or pork

2 tablespoons lemon juice

1 tablespoon grated onion

$1/4$ teaspoon ground ginger

$1/4$ teaspoon turmeric

1 heaped teaspoon ground cumin

1 level teaspoon coriander seeds,
   roughly ground

1 tablespoon finely chopped fresh
   flat-leaf parsley

2 tablespoons olive oil

Paprika and sherry marinade for venison and beef

$1^1/2$ tablespoons Pedro Ximénez
   sherry or sweet oloroso

2 teaspoons sherry vinegar

2 bay leaves, finely chopped or
   crumbled

1 pinch of thyme, fresh or dried

5 grates of nutmeg

$1/2$ teaspoon finely chopped fresh
   rosemary

$1/2$ teaspoon hot paprika, preferably
   smoked

2 garlic cloves, crushed

1 level teaspoon salt

3 tablespoons olive oil

For a basic Spanish chicken and rabbit marinade see page 246.

To make your marinade, combine all the ingredients except the olive oil in the small bowl of a food processor and purée until smooth. Now prepare the meat ready for cooking on the grill:

• spatchcock quail or poussins (i.e. split in half and flatten)
• joint or bone a chicken, or keep it whole and spatchcock it
• trim the skin off a boned leg of lamb, about 1.5kg in weight, open out the leg to make a flat, vaguely rectangular slab of meat, then trim off any silvery sinew and excessive fat. Leave it whole or you can divide it into 4 pieces or dice it into 3cm cubes for shish kebabs
• cut 2 racks of lamb into 14 chops (leave the fat on – it is delicious when charred and crispy).

Toss the meat in the marinade to coat thoroughly, add the olive oil and refrigerate from 4 hours up to 2 days for the flavours to infuse and develop. Remove from the fridge 2 hours before cooking, then season and grill or roast to your liking.

Chicken with spring garlic and Pedro Ximénez

In April we get the first of the new season's garlic from Egypt. The cloves are small but we don't peel them, as much of the outer casing is still tender and juicy. New season's English garlic will be around from June, and again if you pick it slightly immature you can use it skins and all. If you cannot get good 'wet' garlic to use in this recipe, substitute 2 bunches of spring onions, chopped in 2cm lengths, and 6 large, unpeeled garlic cloves, which should be simmered in the olive oil and removed before you brown the chicken.

The vinegar in this dish is just to stop the Pedro Ximénez being too sickly, so if a drier sherry is used, less vinegar will be required.

Serves 4

6 tablespoons olive oil

1 organic or free-range chicken,
   jointed into 8 pieces

4 large heads of wet new season's
   garlic, outer skin removed,
   broken into individual cloves and
   roughly chopped

$1/_2$ teaspoon fennel seeds

2 fresh bay leaves

100ml Pedro Ximénez sherry (or
   sweet cream sherry)

100ml water

2 tablespoons sherry or Montilla
   vinegar, to taste

Set a large (25cm) saucepan over a high heat and add the oil. Season the chicken pieces with salt and then brown them thoroughly until golden on all sides, skin-side first. Do this in 2 batches, starting with the breast pieces. When they are done, remove them and start the leg pieces – it will take about 10-15 minutes for each batch. Once the leg pieces are a rich golden colour, shuffle them to one side of the pan and add the spring garlic, fennel seeds and bay, along with some salt and pepper. Reduce the heat to medium and sauté for about 5-10 minutes, until the garlic has softened. Pour in the sweet sherry and boil for a couple of minutes to get rid of the alcohol. Now add the water and sherry vinegar and place the breast pieces of chicken on top of the rest. Cover with a lid and simmer gently for 15 minutes, until the thickest part of the breast is cooked. Taste for seasoning and serve, steaming hot, with mashed potatoes.

La caldereta

This slow-roast dish from Extremadura is very evocative of the hearty meals served in *ventas* (roadside restaurants) in Spain. The herbs should mimic the vegetation that the Extremaduran sheep and goats graze on. When finished, the meat should be caramelised and sticky on the outside and falling off the bone.

Serves 4–5

1 shoulder of lamb or kid, about 2kg in weight

3 teaspoons fine sea salt

1 tablespoon fresh thyme leaves

1 tablespoon finely chopped fresh rosemary

5 tablespoons olive oil

1 large onion, roughly sliced

18 garlic cloves, skin on

2 bay leaves, preferably fresh

$1/2$ teaspoon fennel seeds

$1/2$ teaspoon smoked sweet paprika

$1/2$ bottle of Spanish white wine

3 tablespoons brandy (optional)

1kg medium-sized firm or waxy potatoes, peeled, quartered and rubbed with $1/2$ teaspoon salt

Rub the shoulder of lamb or kid with the fine sea salt and half the thyme and rosemary and let it stand on a plate for 20 minutes–1 hour.

Preheat the oven to 175°C/350°F/Gas 4.

Put the olive oil, onion, garlic and a pinch of salt in a large roasting tray. Fry for about 10 minutes over a medium heat until the onion softens and starts to colour. Stir in the bay leaves, fennel seeds, paprika and remaining thyme and rosemary, followed by the wine and the brandy, if using. Place the shoulder on top, skin-side up, and put the tray in the oven. Roast for $2^1/2$ hours, basting the shoulder at least 4 times (be careful not to leave any onion on top of the shoulder, lest it burns). At this point, toss the potatoes in the juices in the roasting tray. Turn the oven up to 220°C/425°F/Gas 7 and cook for a further 40 minutes, adding a splash of water to the pan if the juices have totally dried up. Taste for seasoning and leave to rest for at least 10 minutes before serving.

Pan-fried pork with almonds and fennel

We made this dish up at home without much thought, yet agreed it was good enough to be included in this book. The sweet, velvety onions go well with the rich, crunchy almond, while the fennel adds a subtle fragrance. The dish doesn't really need another vegetable, apart from maybe a green salad with a sherry vinegar dressing.

Serves 4

4 red onions (about 450g), cut
    Chinese style (see below)
600g free-range or organic pork fillet
2 small garlic cloves
$1/2$ heaped teaspoon fennel seeds
1 dessertspoon sweet red wine
    vinegar, such as Forum (or use
    any good-quality red wine
    vinegar and a pinch of sugar)
$1/2$ rounded teaspoon smoked hot
    paprika

7 tablespoons (105ml) olive oil
1 fennel bulb, finely chopped
2 bay leaves
50ml white wine
100g blanched almonds, roasted
    and coarsely chopped
1 small bunch (about 20g) of flat-leaf
    parsley, roughly chopped
2 sprigs of young fennel tops, chopped

When we prepare onions for most of our cooking, we slice them across the grain to allow them to soften as much as possible and become part of the background of the dish. Occasionally, we want the visual and textural impact of the onion at the forefront of the dish, and then we cut it Chinese style, along the grain (especially when we use the fresh onions available between spring and early autumn). To do this, halve and peel your onions, trimming away all of the hard root end. Slice them into 5–10mm wedges along the grain. This makes a big difference to the end result.

Trim any sinew from the pork fillet and slice it into medallions 2–3cm thick. Using the flat of your knife blade, gently flatten each one into a disc 1cm thick. Pound the garlic and fennel seeds in a mortar and pestle with a little salt and pepper until smooth, then add the vinegar, paprika and 1 tablespoon of the olive oil. Rub a little of this paste into each slice of pork and set aside.

Add the remaining 6 tablespoons of oil to a wide frying pan and heat over a medium–high flame. Add the onions, fennel, bay leaves and a pinch of salt and cook, stirring regularly, for about 15–20 minutes, until the onions are soft and beginning to caramelise. Remove them with a slotted spoon, leaving as much of the oil behind as possible. Season the pork medallions with salt and pepper, add to the pan and fry for 1–2 minutes on each side, leaving them rare in the middle (fry only one layer in the pan at a time; you may need to do this in 2 batches). Now increase the heat to maximum, return the onions to the pan and add the white wine. Let it boil for a few minutes, until there is no longer a strong smell of alcohol (by which time the pork should be cooked through too). Toss with the almonds, parsley and fennel tops, taste for seasoning and serve immediately.

Venison with peppers and crispy potatoes

In an un-cheffy sort of way, we are not madly keen on rare lamb or beef, but venison is different, for it has a finer texture and is naturally leaner. We are usually prompted to cook dishes such as this in the autumn, either when we get a phone call from one of our game suppliers, Yorkshire Game, to say venison is abundant. This is, in fact, three separate recipes but at Moro they are always served together, along with some watercress, to make a very satisfying plate.

Serves 4

3 tablespoons olive oil

4 thick venison steaks (or loin, entrecote or fillet of beef)

1 quantity of Paprika and Sherry Marinade (see page 237)

1 quantity of Fried Piquillo Peppers with Thyme (page 162)

1 quantity of Crispy Potatoes (page 186)

Ideally, we like to marinate the venison for 3 hours at room temperature.

Heat a frying pan over a medium to high heat. Add the olive oil, venison and all the marinade. Season with salt and fry for a few minutes, until pleasantly brown all over and rare to medium-rare inside, depending on how you like your meat. Turn off the heat, cover loosely with foil and leave to relax for 5 minutes.

When you are ready to eat, place the venison on warm plates. Add a splash of hot water to the pan, give it a good stir and spread the sauce over the venison. Serve with the piquillo peppers and crispy potatoes on the side, plus a watercress salad dressed with olive oil and lemon juice.

Grilled marinated rabbit

In Barcelona, we once chanced upon a small café full of Spanish people spilling out on to the street. We instinctively knew this place had to be good. And it was. We shared a plate of grilled rabbit with chips, simply called *conil* (Catalan for rabbit). The rabbit arrived piping-hot. It had been marinated in thyme, garlic, parsley and white wine, then grilled slowly so the outside was caramelised, the inside juicy and tender. You could easily substitute chicken for the rabbit. We serve this with Almond Alioli.

Serves 4

1 large or 2 small rabbits

1 quantity of Almond Alioli
   (page 274)

lemon wedges, to serve (optional)

Marinade

3 garlic cloves, crushed to a paste
   with a pinch of salt

150ml white wine

3 tablespoons fresh thyme leaves

2 tablespoons olive oil

freshly ground black pepper

To prepare the rabbit, first joint it. Cut the legs and shoulders from the carcass and pull out the liver (be sure to marinate and use the liver, which is delicious). Trim the scrawny ends from the saddle, then use a pair of kitchen scissors or poultry shears to trim the ribcage. Cut the saddle into 4 pieces for a large rabbit, 2 for a small one.

Make the marinade by combining all the ingredients in a blender or food processor and whizzing until emulsified. Place the pieces of rabbit in a large mixing bowl and pour over the marinade. Rub the marinade all over each piece, making sure none is missed. Leave to marinate for at least 6 hours – preferably overnight. Toss a couple of times to ensure all the meat is well flavoured.

Preheat a grill, griddle or barbecue.

Before you grill the rabbit pieces, drain them and season well with salt. Cook under a very hot grill or on a griddle or barbecue, basting with the remaining marinade. Put the legs and shoulders on first, which will take about 10 minutes on each side. When you turn them, add the saddle (which will need about 10 minutes, turning once). About 5 minutes before the meat is done, put the liver, which cooks fastest of all, on the grill.

Serve with sautéed or fried potatoes, braised chard or salad and the almond alioli, plus lemon wedges, if you wish.

Chicken and prawn romesco

This is a Catalan dish, with its typical marriage of *mar y terra*, from sea and land. At Moro, after years of burning untold kilos of almonds when trying to roast them, we now acquire salted roasted almonds for this dish. We advise you to do the same.

In Spain large, locally caught prawns (*cigalas*) or langoustines would probably be used. Often we don't have that luxury, unless we get them specially from Scotland, so we use cooked North Atlantic prawns, frozen with the shells on, which have an excellent flavour.

Serves 4

350g cooked shell-on North Atlantic prawns (about 40), or about 400g langoustines

1 medium chicken (1.5–1.7kg), free-range or organic, jointed into 8 pieces (skin on)

6 tablespoons olive oil

6 garlic cloves, thinly sliced

1 medium onion, finely chopped

3 dried ñoras peppers, seeded, chopped and soaked in boiling water for 10 minutes (or use 1 dessertspoon sweet smoked paprika)

300g flavoursome tomatoes, blanched, peeled, seeded and finely chopped

1 bay leaf

4 tablespoons brandy (or oloroso sherry)

75g salted roasted almonds

4 tablespoons finely chopped fresh flat-leaf parsley

Peel just over half the prawns. Use the prawn shells to make a little light stock with 600ml water, adding some stock vegetables if you like – just boil for 10 minutes, then strain and set aside.

Season the chicken pieces with salt and pepper. Heat 2 tablespoons of the olive oil in a wide saucepan over a medium heat, add the chicken (in batches if necessary) and brown for 5–10 minutes on each side. Meanwhile, heat the remaining oil over a medium-low heat in another, smaller saucepan, add the sliced garlic and fry until crisp and golden (take care not to let it burn). Remove the garlic with a slotted spoon and set aside, but leave the pan on the heat. Add the onion and a pinch of salt, increase the heat to medium and fry for about 15 minutes, until the onion is soft, sweet and golden brown. Add the ñoras peppers (or paprika) and fry for 1 minute more. Remove.

When the chicken is browned, transfer the sweet onion and peppers to the wide saucepan and add the tomatoes, bay leaf and brandy. Simmer until the alcohol has boiled off. Measure out 400ml of the prawn stock, add it to the pan and let it bubble gently for about 15 minutes, or until the chicken is done.

Make a picada by crushing the crispy garlic and roast almonds together in a mortar and pestle or in a food processor, until they have the texture of coarse breadcrumbs. Stir the picada into the chicken mixture and let it cook for a few minutes more, just to thicken. Remove from the heat and stir in the prawns. Leave for a minute or two for the prawns to heat through, then stir in the parsley and serve.

Grilled poussins with zaatar

This recipe is also delicious with a roast chicken, or roast partridge when in season. At Moro, we serve it accompanied by Fried Potatoes with Coriander, Tahini Sauce and watercress dressed with olive oil and lemon. If you can't get hold of zaatar, then make your own simple version: mix $1^1/_2$ teaspoons of dried oregano and $1^1/_2$ teaspoons of dried thyme with 2 tablespoons of sesame seeds.

Serves 4

4 poussins, spatchcocked (split open and flattened) by your butcher

1 large garlic clove

1 tablespoon fresh thyme leaves

$^1/_2$ teaspoon sea salt

1 tablespoon lemon juice

3 rounded tablespoons zaatar

3 tablespoons olive oil

To serve

1 quantity of Tahini Sauce (page 265)

2 tablespoons zaatar

1 lemon in half or quarters

1 quantity of Fried Potatoes with Coriander (page 185)

150g watercress, lightly dressed with olive oil and lemon

A few hours or the day before, marinate the poussins: crush the garlic and thyme with the salt, then stir in the lemon juice, zaatar, oil and some black pepper. Rub this over the flattened insides of the birds, trying not to get too much on the skin. Leave to marinate.

The next day, preheat a barbecue or large griddle pan. If using a barbecue, the trick is to cook on it just as the coals start to burn down, when it is still hot but the heat is just beginning to wane. If using a griddle pan, get it very hot but turn the heat down as soon as the birds hit the pan. In either case, season the poussins on both sides with salt and pepper, then grill them for 10–15 minutes on the skin side and about 10 minutes on the other. The flesh should be opaque all the way through but still juicy. Serve with the tahini sauce drizzled over and sprinkled with zaatar, with the lemon, watercress and potatoes on the side.

Pigeon salad with figs and pomegranates

Many cuttings have been taken from Hassan's black fig tree, one of which we are lucky enough to have, so last year the allotment was awash with the most incredible figs. In this salad we sear them so they caramelise, which is a delicious combination with the gaminess of the pigeon.

Serves 4

1 quantity of Pomegranate
    Molasses Marinade (see page 236)

8 plump, skinless pigeon breasts
3 tablespoons olive oil
4 figs, skins on but cleaned with a
    damp cloth and cut in halves or
    quarters

4 handfuls of watercress or a
    mixture of frisée and other salad
200g (drained weight) cooked
    chickpeas, warmed for the salad

Dressing

1 tablespoon lemon juice
1 tablespoon pomegranate molasses
    or 3 tablespoons fresh
    pomegranate juice (see page 52)

3 tablespoons extra virgin olive oil

Rub the pomegranate molasses marinade over the pigeon breasts and leave to infuse for a few hours. For the dressing, whisk all the ingredients together, season with salt and pepper and set aside.

When you are ready to serve the salad, place a large frying pan over a medium heat and add 2 tablespoons of the olive oil. When it is hot, add the pigeon breasts, seasoned with salt and pepper, and fry for 2–3 minutes on one side. Turn over and continue to fry for 3 minutes, until juicy and still slightly pink. Remove the pigeon from the pan and set aside to rest.

Meanwhile, heat the remaining tablespoon of olive oil in the pan, add the figs and fry until slightly soft and jammy. Dress the salad and toss well with the warm chickpeas. Spread the salad on 4 large plates and top with the figs, sliced pigeon breasts and any pan juices. Serve immediately.

Roast chicken with sumac, onions and pine nuts

Chicken roasted with sumac is Lebanese in origin. Sumac is a red powder ground from a berry and is lemony in flavour.

Serves 4

4 tablespoons olive oil

1 medium organic or free-range
   chicken (1.5–1.7kg), jointed into
   8 pieces (leave the skin on)

6 small new season's onions whole,
   (or 12 spring onions), sliced in
   2cm lengths

2 tablespoons sumac

50g pine nuts

3 tablespoons water

Preheat the oven to 220°C/425°F/Gas 7.

Heat 3 tablespoons of the oil in a wide (30cm) ovenproof frying pan over a medium-high heat. Season the chicken pieces with salt and pepper and brown them thoroughly on all sides, skin-side first. Remove the chicken from the pan and pour off the fat. Put the onions in the still-hot pan and sprinkle with half the sumac, the remaining tablespoon of oil and some salt and pepper. Arrange the pieces of chicken on top, skin-side up, and sprinkle with the pine nuts and the remaining sumac. Put the pan over a medium heat for 5 minutes to get the onions going, then transfer to the oven. Roast for 15–20 minutes, until the chicken is cooked. Transfer the chicken to a serving dish, add the water to the onions to make a chunky sauce, and pour it over the chicken.

Chicken with almonds and grapes

This is another incarnation of our ground almond fetish. Jolly good it is too.

Serves 4

100g whole blanched almonds

4 teaspoons sherry vinegar

400ml water

4 tablespoons olive oil

8 garlic cloves, skins on

1 organic or free-range chicken,
    jointed into 8 pieces

2 fresh bay leaves

40 seedless white grapes, preferably
    muscat

100ml light white wine, or muscatel
    sherry

Grind the almonds as finely as possible in a food processor – let the machine run for 5–10 minutes, stopping to push the almonds down if they ride up the side of the bowl. Then with the motor still running, slowly add the vinegar and 250ml of the water splash by splash until the almonds have a smooth, creamy consistency. Set aside.

Place a large frying pan over a medium heat and add the olive oil. When it is hot but not smoking, add the garlic cloves and fry for 3 minutes on either side, until slightly golden. Remove the garlic and set aside. Now season the chicken with salt, put it in the pan skin-side down and increase the heat slightly. Fry for about 5–10 minutes, until the skin has a good golden colour and is fairly crisp – take care, as the chicken can spit. Turn over the chicken pieces and cook for another 5–10 minutes, until golden on the other side. Return the garlic to the pan with the bay leaves and grapes and fry for half a minute. Then add the white wine and boil for a minute, shaking the pan to emulsify the sauce. Reduce the heat to low and simmer for 5–10 minutes, taking out any breast meat if it is cooked and putting it to one side. After another 5 minutes or so, when the brown meat is tender, stir in the almond purée. Return any breast meat to the pan and simmer for a couple of minutes more, gradually adding the remaining 150ml of water as required by the thickening sauce – the consistency should be no thicker than double cream. Leave to rest for a moment, then taste for seasoning and serve with some simple greens – sprouting broccoli, spring greens or chard would be lovely.

Roast pork loin with pomegranates

The long history of the Moors in Spain had a significant influence on the cooking of Andalucía. When the Moors were finally expelled from Spain at the end of the sixteenth century, the eating of pork was actively encouraged. This might explain the unusual presence of Moorish flavours (pomegranate) in a pork dish. Try to use fresh juice or the commercial variety Pom, which has a very good concentrated flavour. Failing that, use pomegranate molasses diluted with water.

Serves 4–6

1 piece of organic or free-range
    pork loin on the bone, about 1.5kg
2 teaspoons fine sea salt
1 small garlic clove
$1/2$ heaped teaspoon fennel seeds,
    roughly ground
$1/2$ teaspoon finely ground cinnamon
1 tablespoon fresh thyme leaves
1 tablespoon olive oil

75g fresh pomegranate seeds
    (equivalent to 1 small or $1/2$ large
    pomegranate)
2 tablespoons finely chopped fresh
    flat-leaf parsley
150ml pomegranate juice – squeeze
    the seeds of about 1–2
    pomegranates by hand (page 52)
    or use Pom pomegranate juice

Preheat the oven to 230°C/450°F/Gas 8.

Score the skin of the pork with a very sharp knife, making parallel incisions no more than 1cm apart and about 5mm deep, cutting through the skin and fat but not the flesh (you could ask your butcher to do this). Rub half the salt into the skin of the pork, working it into the cuts, then rub the remaining salt into the flesh side. Crush the garlic, fennel seeds, cinnamon, thyme and olive oil to a paste and rub it into the flesh side of the meat, taking care not to get it on the skin, where it would burn.

Place the pork in a roasting tray just large enough to accommodate it and leave to stand for half an hour, then place in the oven. It should take about 1 hour and 10 minutes to cook. Remove it when a meat thermometer inserted in the centre registers 60°C, or when the tip of a skewer inserted in it feels uncomfortably warm when touched to your lip. Leave the joint to rest, loosely covered with foil, for 15–20 minutes.

When you are ready to serve, put the joint on a carving board and pour off any excess fat from the baking tray. Put the tray over a medium heat and add the pomegranate juice, stirring to deglaze the pan. Season with salt and pepper. Carve the joint, pour the gravy over and scatter with the pomegranate seeds and parsley. Delicious with roast fennel and potatoes.

Duck fattee with chickpea pilaf, pomegranates, aubergines and walnuts

Fit for a king, this is an elaborate and celebratory dish, but well worth the effort so we urge you to give it a go. We often serve this at Christmas at Moro, as it feels so festive. It really pays off to get a damn good duck and roast it in style.

Serves 8

1 Barbary or Gressingham duck,
    weighing about 2.5kg
1 dessertspoon fine sea salt
$1/_4$ heaped teaspoon ground cinnamon

seeds of 1 large pomegranate (about
    150–175g seeds) – squeeze half the
    seeds to make juice (see page 52)

Crispbread
25g unsalted butter

2 pitta breads

Chickpea pilaf
75g unsalted butter
4cm piece of cinnamon stick
$1/_2$ large onion, thinly sliced
300g basmati rice, soaked in tepid
    water for 1 hour

400g tin of chickpeas, drained
450ml light chicken stock

Fried aubergine
1 large or 2 medium aubergines,
    cut into 2cm cubes

1 teaspoon fine sea salt
6 tablespoons olive oil

To layer up the fattee
500g good-quality Greek yoghurt,
    such as Total, mixed with 6
    tablespoons water and $1/_2$ crushed
    garlic clove
1 medium bunch (about 30g) of flat-
    leaf parsley, leaves picked

75g walnuts, broken roughly
seeds of a large pomegranate (about
    150–175g seeds)

Preheat the oven to 230°C/450°F/Gas 8.

To roast the duck, dry the skin with a tea towel and remove the giblets. Rub the skin with the sea salt and ground cinnamon and place breast-side down on a rack in a roasting tray. Roast for 20 minutes, then turn over and roast for 20 minutes on the other side. Turn the oven down to 180°C/350°F/Gas 4 and roast for a further 2 hours.

While the duck is roasting, prepare the crispbread. Melt the butter over a low heat. As it is melting, warm the pitta in the oven for a couple of minutes, then carefully split each bread open into two halves and brush the butter on both sides. Place the halves on a rack on the middle shelf of the oven and bake for 15–20 minutes, until golden.

For the chickpea pilaf, heat the butter with the cinnamon in a medium saucepan until it foams. Add the onion and fry over a medium heat for about 15 minutes, until sweet and golden. Drain the rice well and add it to the onion. Fry for a minute, stirring to coat it in the butter, then add the chickpeas and chicken stock, along with a good pinch of salt. Cover with a circle of grease-proof paper and a tight-fitting lid and boil for 5 minutes. Reduce the heat to a gentle simmer and cook for 5 minutes more. Remove from the heat and leave to rest, covered, for at least 10 minutes before serving.

Toss the aubergine cubes with the sea salt and leave in a colander for 20 minutes. Pat dry with kitchen paper. Heat the olive oil in a wide frying pan or a large wok over a high flame. Add the aubergine cubes and fry for about 15 minutes, until soft and brown. Place on kitchen paper to blot any excess oil. Keep warm.

When the duck is cooked, remove it from the oven, place on a carving board and pour off any excess fat from the roasting tray. Put the tray over a medium heat and pour in the pomegranate juice, stirring to deglaze. Season with salt and pepper.

At this stage, it is just a question of layering things up on one or more big platters or serving dishes. Everything needs to be hot apart from the crispbread and yoghurt. The duck needs to be carved into small pieces, breast off the bone, the thighs in half, then it can be gently warmed in the oven if necessary, but try to time it so it stays hot and crisp.

The order to layer your plate is first half the crispbread, broken by hand into pieces, then the pilaf, then the duck, then the aubergine, then a drizzling of the pomegranate sauce, then the remaining crispbread, the yoghurt and finally lots of parsley leaves, the walnuts and the pomegranate seeds. Eat right away – a feast on a plate.

Sauces

Salmorejo sauce

Best known as a classic cold Cordoban soup, this is also served as a fresh and zingy summer sauce which is fantastic with chicken, fish or fried aubergines or as part of a salad (see page 74).

Serves 4

1 garlic clove, crushed to a paste
   with a pinch of salt
500g sweet, ripe tomatoes, cut in half
50g crustless white bread
5 tablespoons extra virgin olive oil

1 tablespoon good-quality sweet red
   wine vinegar, such as Forum, or
   sherry vinegar
1–2 teaspoons sugar (optional)

Using a handheld blender or a food processor, purée all the ingredients except the sugar until completely smooth. The sauce should have the consistency of apple purée. Strain through a sieve if not sufficiently smooth. Season to taste with the sugar (only necessary if the tomatoes are not so sweet themselves) and some salt and pepper. Chill immediately, and taste for seasoning once more just before serving.

Beetroot borani

Boranis are refreshing yoghurt drinks from Iran, so are not strictly speaking our domain, yet the flavours seemed so right for us we just had to use them. At Moro we serve this as a sauce to accompany chicken or white fish (to serve 8) or thinned slightly and chilled as a soup (to serve 3–4).

500g raw beetroot
400g good-quality Greek yoghurt,
   such as Total
2 tablespoons olive oil
1 garlic clove, crushed to a paste
   with $^{1}/_{2}$ teaspoon salt

a pinch of sugar (optional)
1 small bunch (about 20g) of dill,
   finely chopped

Boil the beetroot, skins on, until tender (this takes quite a while, about 1–1$^1/_2$ hours). Drain, then peel them by hand under cold running water and transfer to a food processor. Purée the beetroot to obtain a smooth paste, then add the yoghurt, olive oil, garlic and sugar and blitz until very smooth. Transfer to a bowl, stir in the dill and season to taste with salt and pepper.

Green herb borani

Wonderfully fresh and fragrant, superb with a cold roast chicken, boiled beet-root and potato salad.

Serves 4–6

1 small bunch (about 10g) of dill, leaves picked

1 medium bunch (about 20g) of sorrel

a few sprigs (about 5g) of mint, leaves picked

1 small bunch (about 10g) of tarragon, leaves picked

1 small bunch (about 15g) of flat-leaf parsley, leaves picked

50g spinach, blanched, refreshed in cold water and drained

1 spring onion, cut in 3cm lengths

1 garlic clove, crushed to a paste with 1 scant teaspoon fine sea salt

2 tablespoons extra virgin olive oil

400g good-quality Greek yoghurt, such as Total

Wash the herbs and let them drip dry (don't spin them – you need a little water to remain). Put the herbs, spinach, spring onion and garlic in a food processor and purée until smooth. Add the oil and yoghurt and process until they are incorporated. Transfer to a bowl and season to taste with salt and pepper.

Tahini sauce

Serves 4

$^1/_2$ garlic clove, crushed to a smooth paste with a pinch of salt

$2^1/_2$ tablespoons tahini

1 tablespoon extra virgin olive oil

1 tablespoon lemon juice

6–8 tablespoons water

Combine the garlic, tahini and olive oil in a small bowl. Add the lemon juice, then whisk in the water a tablespoonful at a time, stirring briskly between additions to ensure a smooth sauce. The consistency should be between single and double cream. Season to taste with salt and pepper.

Tahini, walnut and chilli sauce

We happily eat this sauce with simply cooked white fish, chicken or lamb.

Serves 4

50g walnut halves, broken up
   slightly
3 tablespoons vegetable oil
2 tablespoons finely chopped mildish
   red chilli

1 tablespoon finely chopped flat-leaf
   parsley
1 quantity of Tahini Sauce (page 265)

Fry the walnuts in the vegetable oil until they start to brown, then drain immediately lest they burn, discarding the oil. Stir the walnuts, chilli and parsley into the tahini sauce.

Walnut tarator

Perhaps the most classic of Turkish tarators, but another favourite is a version made with pine nuts instead.

Serves 4

150g walnuts
1 garlic clove, crushed to a paste
   with a pinch of salt
$1/2$ teaspoon ground allspice

3 tablespoons olive oil
$1^1/2$ tablespoons red wine vinegar
4 tablespoons water

Grind the nuts quite finely in a mortar and pestle or food processor, then add the garlic and allspice. Combine the olive oil with the vinegar and water and gradually mix them into the walnuts to make a white, aromatic emulsified sauce with the consistency of thin mayonnaise; add a little more water if necessary. Season to taste with salt and pepper.

Mojo rojo

We can't pretend to know much about this Canary Island sauce but we know we like it. In the past we have talked about 'the language of spice', meaning you can read cultural influences through the spices or ingredients. This mojo could almost be a chilli sauce from North Africa or the Eastern Mediterranean, but the use of bay, wine vinegar and smoked paprika anchor it to Spain.

Serves 4–6

1 large red pepper

6 large red chillies

15g crustless white bread, broken into large crumbs

7 tablespoons (105ml) extra virgin olive oil

2 fresh bay leaves, stalks removed

2 garlic cloves, peeled

1 teaspoon ground cumin

1 tablespoon sweet red wine vinegar, such as Forum (or use any good-quality red wine vinegar with a pinch of sugar)

$^{1}/_{2}$ teaspoon smoked sweet paprika

Grill the pepper and half the chillies until soft and blackened, then peel and seed them. Seed the remaining raw chillies and chop them finely.

Fry the bread in half the olive oil until golden and crisp. Combine the bread, its oil, the chillies (both raw and cooked) and the red pepper in a food processor with the bay, garlic, cumin, vinegar and a pinch of salt and purée until smooth. Transfer to a bowl and add the remaining oil, mixed with the paprika. Stir to combine, season with salt, and thin with 1–2 tablespoons of water, as required.

Mojo verde

This is the green version of Mojo Rojo (page 268), which is fantastic with Papas Aruglas (page 186) and roast pork.

Serves 4

1 small (or $^1/_2$ large) green pepper, seeded and roughly chopped

100g large green chillies, seeded and roughly chopped

2 garlic cloves, peeled

1 small bunch (about 20g) of coriander, stalks and all, roughly chopped

1 teaspoon ground cumin

1 teaspoon dried oregano

1 tablespoon sweet red wine vinegar, such as Forum (or use any good-quality red wine vinegar with a pinch of sugar)

4 tablespoons extra virgin olive oil

Combine the green pepper and chillies in a food processor with the garlic, coriander, cumin, oregano and a good pinch of salt and purée until quite fine. Transfer to a bowl, stir in the vinegar and oil and taste for seasoning.

Harissa

This recipe is lifted from our previous book, *Casa Moro*, but it is such an essential sauce in our repertoire that we have included it here too.

Serves 6–8

250g fresh, long red chillies

3 heaped teaspoons caraway seeds, ground

2 heaped teaspoons cumin seeds, ground

1 teaspoon black cumin seeds, ground (optional)

3 garlic cloves

100g piquillo peppers (or roasted and peeled red peppers)

1 dessertspoon tomato purée

1 dessertspoon red wine vinegar

4 tablespoons olive oil

2 level teaspoons smoked paprika

Slice the tops off the chillies, then halve them lengthways. Lay each half on a chopping board, cut-side up, gently scrape away the seeds with a teaspoon and discard them. Blend the chillies in a food processor with a pinch of sea salt, the spices and the garlic cloves until smooth. It is important that the chillies be as pulverised as possible, with no little bits. Add the peppers, tomato purée and vinegar and blend again until very smooth. Transfer to a mixing bowl. Now add the olive oil (it is important to add the oil at this stage, for if you add it to the food processor it will turn the harissa a creamy colour). Sprinkle the paprika on top of the oil and stir in. Taste and season with more salt to balance out the vinegar.

Harissa keeps well in the fridge, but be sure to cover it with a little olive oil to seal it from the air.

Charmoula

The classic Moroccan marinade for fish, prawns or chicken is also good as a sauce.

Serves 4

1 medium bunch (about 40g) of
   coriander
2 large garlic cloves, grated
2 teaspoons ground cumin

2 teaspoons Moroccan paprika
   (or other unsmoked paprika)
$1^1/_2$ teaspoons red wine vinegar
4 tablespoons olive oil

Chop the coriander stalks and leaves finely, keeping them separate. In a mortar and pestle, crush the stalks to a fine paste with the garlic, a good pinch of salt, plus the cumin and paprika, adding the vinegar gradually as you go. Stir in the chopped coriander leaves and oil then check for seasoning.

Tomato sauce

If you grow tomatoes, you will inevitably have a glut towards the end of the summer. We often make this simple tomato sauce, which freezes very well. My sister Rose Prince makes a wonderful tomato sauce and I always struggle to get mine to taste as good. The spices are optional.

Makes about 1 litre

4 garlic cloves, thinly sliced
12 tablespoons (180ml) olive oil
3 medium onions, finely chopped
4cm piece of cinnamon stick
   (optional)

1 tablespoon fine sea salt
1 teaspoon ground cumin (optional)
2kg ripe tomatoes, blanched and
   peeled

Fry the garlic in 4 tablespoons of the oil until nut–brown (but not burnt) and set aside. Heat the remaining oil in a large saucepan, add the onions, cinnamon and sea salt and fry over a medium heat for 30 minutes or until sweet and golden, stirring occasionally. Add the cumin, cook for 2 minutes more, then add the tomatoes, the fried garlic and its oil. Bring to a boil and simmer for half an hour, mashing a little with a potato masher. The sauce is ready as soon as it starts to thicken and all the tomatoes have broken down, but you could cook it longer if you prefer a more reduced sauce. Season with pepper, and salt if it needs it, and strain out some of the tomato seeds if they bother you (they don't bother us).

Almond alioli

A nutty, garlicky mayonnaise which is great with chicken, rabbit and fish alike.

Serves 4

50g whole blanched almonds   2 organic egg yolks
2 garlic cloves   250ml extra virgin olive oil
Maldon sea salt   250ml sunflower oil
a good squeeze of lemon

Preheat the oven to 150°C/300°F/Gas 2. Spread the almonds out on a baking sheet and toast them in the oven for about 20 minutes until golden. Leave to cool, then chop roughly.

Crush the garlic cloves in a mortar and pestle with a pinch of Maldon salt. When smooth, add the lemon juice. At this point, you can transfer the garlic to a mixing bowl, if you prefer, add the egg yolks, then whisk in the oil drop by drop with a balloon whisk. Otherwise, continue in the mortar and pestle: add the egg yolks and stir to break the membrane. Continue stirring while you add the oil, almost painfully slowly at first – that is, drop by drop – then with more confidence when you see that a thick emulsion has formed. When all the oil has been incorporated, stir in the almonds, then season to taste with more salt and lemon juice if necessary.

Puddings

Asure – Noah's pudding

We made Noah's pudding in the early days at Moro. It is a delicately fragrant and textured fruit compote. The story goes that when the Flood had subsided and the animals had wandered away, this pudding was made with all the grains, pulses and dried fruit left in the store of the Ark. We had slightly forgotten about this dish until recently, as we felt it was too substantial to end a meal. However, we were reminded of it by Adile, our lovely Turkish neighbour. She has a big jar of it in her shed, which she uses as a power food to keep her going throughout the day. We would recommend making a large batch to serve with yoghurt for breakfast, as a snack, or pudding after a light meal.

Serves 15

100g pearl barley	50g pine nuts
2 tablespoons short–grain rice	50g blanched almonds
1 orange	50g walnuts
50g sultanas	50g sesame seeds
50g currants	120g cooked white beans or chickpeas,
100g dried apricots, quartered	drained and rinsed (optional)
100g dried figs, quartered	200g caster sugar
10cm piece of cinnamon stick	100g honey
50g shelled raw pistachios	2 tablespoons rosewater

To serve (per portion)

1 tablespoon pomegranate seeds	4 walnut halves

Simmer the barley and rice in 8 litres of water for 3 hours over a very low heat, covering the pan with a close–fitting lid. Meanwhile, use a sharp knife to cut the peel (and the pith) from the orange. Dice the peel and flesh in 1cm cubes. Cover the dried fruits with 500ml cold water and leave to soak.

Once the grains have simmered and started to break down, add the dried fruits, along with their soaking liquor, and all the other ingredients except the rosewater. Simmer, still covered, for 30 minutes. Remove from the heat, stir in the rosewater and leave to cool, then chill. When it is cold, the consistency should be like a thick soup – if it sets too solid, stir in a little water. Keep this in the fridge for up to 4 days and serve in small bowls as required, sprinkled with pomegranate seeds and walnuts.

Poached cherries with almond cream

When grinding almonds in a food processor, whether it be for *ajo blanco* or this almond cream, there is a wonderful eureka moment when the almonds stop smelling like old sawdust and the aroma is transformed into warm almond essence. This is how we make marzipan as well. Our fantastic head chef David Cook came up with this recipe and it has become this year's favourite.

Serves 4

200g blanched almonds
200g caster sugar
450ml water

500g cherries (pitted if you like)
5 strips of lemon zest, taken with a
    potato peeler

Grind the almonds in a food processor with half the sugar until super-fine – leaving the machine running for several minutes. Gradually add the water, very slowly at first to get the paste as fine as possible. Transfer the white cream to a bowl, cover with cling film and refrigerate.

Put the cherries (we normally leave the stones in) in a saucepan with 300ml water, the remaining sugar and the strips of lemon zest. Bring to a simmer and cook for a couple of minutes, until the liquor is dark red and the cherries tender. Chill the poached cherries before serving them over the almond pudding.

Rhubarb and rosewater fool

Although we change our starters and main courses a lot on the menu, our puddings remain Moro classics like the yoghurt cake and the chocolate and apricot tart. Coming up with new puddings for *Moro East*, we are indebted to our tester, Jacob Kenedy, whose brilliant training and knowledge turned our ideas into real recipes. The addition of rosewater to this favourite fool gives it a subtle, exotic fragrance.

Serves 4

400g rhubarb, cut in 3cm lengths   350ml double cream
125g caster sugar   1 tablespoon rosewater
50ml water

Preheat the oven to 175°C/350°F/Gas 4.

Toss the rhubarb with 100g of the sugar and the water and spread in a snug roasting tin. Cover loosely with foil and bake until tender – about 30 minutes. Leave to cool in the roasting tin, then refrigerate for an hour or so.

Mix the cream with the remaining sugar and the rosewater and whip until it forms firm peaks. Fold the chilled rhubarb (set any syrup aside) into the cream but don't over-mix. Spoon alternating dollops of cream with spoonfuls of rhubarb syrup into glasses for a marbled look and chill until set. Delicious as is, or scattered with toasted almonds.

Cherry and anis sorbet with lemon biscuits

Serves 4–6

150g caster sugar
150ml water
750g cherries

3 tablespoons sweet anis liqueur (or
    arak or ouzo)
juice of 1 lemon

Lemon biscuits (makes about 45)

150g caster sugar
150g semolina
75g plain flour
150g unsalted butter, diced

grated zest of 2 lemons
1 organic egg
1 organic egg yolk

Combine the sugar, water and 400g of the cherries in a saucepan and bring to a simmer. Cook until the cherries are just soft, then remove from the heat and leave until cool enough to remove the stones. Blend until smooth and pass through a fine sieve. Leave to cool completely, then add the anis liqueur and lemon juice to taste. Freeze in an ice-cream machine according to the manufacturer's instructions. Cut the remaining cherries into eighths, fold them into the sorbet and freeze until set.

To make the biscuits, put the sugar, semolina and flour in a bowl and rub in the butter with your fingertips as if you're making a crumble – or use a mixer fitted with a paddle attachment. Work the mixture just until no lumps of butter remain. Add the lemon zest, egg and egg yolk and stir until thoroughly combined. Wrap in cling film and refrigerate until firm.

Preheat the oven to 160°C/325°F/Gas 3. Line 2 baking sheets with a silicone liner or baking parchment and place teaspoonfuls of the mixture (about the size of a large marble) on it, 8cm apart. Bake for 15 minutes, until golden brown. Leave the biscuits to cool and crisp up before serving with the sorbet.

Mango ice cream

This year has been a fantastic year for the Alphonso mango. When the season approaches in May we badger our vegetable supplier every day to see if he has spotted the first boxes in Spitalfields market. So good are they, that the first taste makes you want to gorge on them. The perfumed flesh is firm, sweet and lemony in equal harmony. At Moro we either serve this simple ice cream or three halves of prepared mango with a few pomegranate seeds scattered on top.

Serves 6–8

600g ripe Alphonso mango flesh
(about 5 Alphonso mangoes,
peeled, stones removed)

juice of 1 lime or lemon
75ml evaporated milk
200ml sweetened condensed milk

Purée all the ingredients together. Push the mixture through a sieve to eliminate any fibres if necessary, then freeze in an ice-cream machine until firm.

Mel y mato

The texture of homemade cheese (mato) is impossible to find in a shop, so it is worth making the effort. Combined with silky honey (mel) and unctuous figs it is a texture sensation.

Serves 4

Lemon mato (curd cheese)
1 litre milk
200ml double cream

grated zest of $^1/_2$ lemon
1 dessertspoon rennet

To serve
100g honeycomb
6 large figs or 8 loquats, halved

50g pine nuts, lightly toasted
a few tiny mint leaves

Heat the milk, cream and lemon zest to blood temperature, then remove from the heat and stir in the rennet. Cover and leave in a warm place for 2 hours, until set like jelly. Cut through the curd with a knife to make 2cm squares. Line a sieve with a fine white napkin or a double layer of muslin. Using a large spoon, gently scoop the curds into the cloth, taking care to break them as little as possible. Leave to drain for 24 hours, after which you should have about 350g creamy curd cheese.

Divide the cheese in 4 and serve each portion with a cube of honeycomb and a few halved fruits. Scatter with the pine nuts and mint leaves and serve immediately.

Almond meringue with anise and raspberries

Serves 4–6

3 organic egg whites

150g caster sugar, plus 2 tablespoons

1 dessertspoon white wine vinegar

100g almonds, roasted and sliced
   by hand

1 dessertspoon anise (or fennel) seeds

300ml whipping cream

400g raspberries

3 tablespoons sweet anis liqueur
   (optional)

Preheat the oven to 120°C/250°F/Gas $^1/_2$.

It is easiest to use an electric whisk to make the meringue. Whisk the egg whites until they foam, then begin adding the 150g sugar a tablespoon or two at a time, whisking constantly at a high speed to achieve a stiff yet supple and glossy meringue. Mix in the vinegar towards the end, when the meringue is almost ready. Finally, fold in two-thirds of the almonds and all the anise.

Spoon the meringue in 4 or 6 billowing mounds on a baking tray lined with baking parchment, then scatter with the remaining almonds. Bake for $1^3/_4$ hours, then turn off the oven and leave the meringue in it, with the door closed, until completely cool – another few hours.

Before serving, whip the cream with the 2 tablespoons of sugar and gently toss the raspberries in the anis liqueur (if using). Serve the meringues with the raspberries and cream on the side.

Poached peaches with cava granizado

The colour of this granizado is as beautiful as the taste.

Serves 6

1 bottle of Cava
500ml water
10cm piece of cinnamon stick
4 cloves
2 strips of orange zest, taken with a
    potato peeler
2 strips of lemon zest, taken with a
    potato peeler

1 bay leaf
200g caster sugar
6 peaches, preferably white (not too
    ripe – it is best when they are
    sweet but still a little firm)

Combine all the ingredients except the peaches in a large saucepan and bring to a simmer. Add the peaches and poach until tender but not mushy – this will take about 5–15 minutes, depending on the ripeness and size of the peaches. Remove the peaches gently, leave to cool slightly, then peel them with your fingers, returning the pink skin to the poaching liquor for colour. Chill the peaches.

Simmer the poaching liquor for 15 minutes, until it has reduced to about 1 litre, then strain through a sieve and pour into a clean baking dish to cool. Place the dish in the freezer and stir every 20–30 minutes with a fork as it freezes, to produce delicate pink crystals of aromatic ice. Serve each peach on top of a mound of granizado.

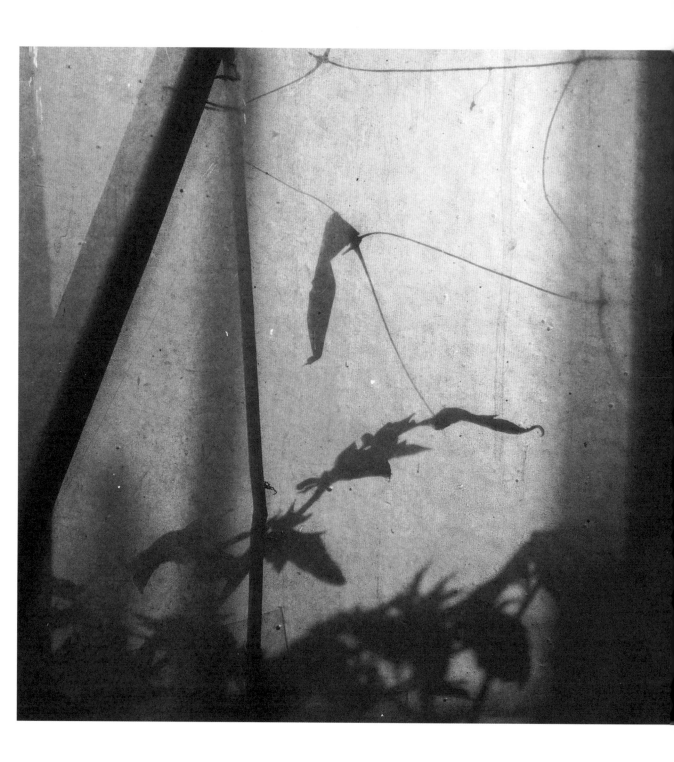

Pine nut and rosewater Tropézienne

This cake is a moorish version of the famous tarte Tropézienne that we used to buy in St Tropez. The rosewater cream is based on a simple crème pâtissière, with rosewater and whipped cream added for aroma and lightness.

Serves 8–10

Brioche dough

1 teaspoon dried yeast (or 10g fresh yeast)	2 organic eggs
	2 organic egg yolks
120ml tepid water	100g unsalted butter, softened at
300g plain flour	room temperature
50g caster sugar	150g pine nuts
$^1/_2$ teaspoon salt	icing sugar for dusting (optional)

Rosewater cream

$^1/_2$ vanilla pod, slit open lengthways	250ml milk
25g cornflour	2 tablespoons rosewater
3 organic egg yolks	40g unsalted butter
100g caster sugar	250ml double cream

First make the brioche. Dissolve the yeast in the water and mix with 100g of the flour. Cover and leave in a warm place until doubled in volume. Sift the sugar, salt and remaining flour into a bowl (as this is quite a wet dough, it is easiest to make in a mixer fitted with a dough hook). Make a well in the centre of the flour and put the whole eggs, 1 egg yolk and the yeast mixture in it. Bring the dough together, knead for a few minutes, then slowly start to incorporate the butter. Once the butter is worked into the dough, knead in two-thirds of the pine nuts. Put the dough in an oiled bowl, cover and leave to rise at room temperature (no warmer than 25°C, or the butter may melt and separate from the dough) for 2 hours or until doubled in bulk.

Grease a 25cm springform cake tin with oil or butter and line the base with baking parchment. Press the dough into the tin, paint it with the last egg yolk and scatter with the remaining pine nuts. Leave to rise, again at room temperature, this time until trebled in bulk – just over 2 hours.

Preheat the oven to 175°C/350°F/Gas 4.

Bake the brioche for 30 minutes, until the nuts and crust are a rich golden brown. Leave to cool before assembling the cake, but bear in mind that this brioche is best eaten on the day of baking.

Next make the rosewater cream. Scrape the seeds from the vanilla pod, reserving the pod, and put them in a mixing bowl with the cornflour, egg yolks and sugar. Beat to a thick paste. Bring the milk to the boil with the vanilla pod, remove the pod, then slowly beat the boiling milk into the egg mixture. Return the mixture to the saucepan and slowly bring back to a simmer, stirring constantly – the mixture will thicken dramatically. Decant the mixture into a bowl, stir in the rosewater and let it cool slightly. When it is about 50–60°C (when you can put your finger in for a second, but not hold it there), stir in the butter. Cover and leave to cool, then chill for a few hours in the fridge.

Whip the cream until firm. Stir the custard to loosen it (it will have set solid), then fold in the whipped cream.

To assemble the cake, cut the brioche horizontally in half to make 2 discs. Pile all the rosewater cream on to the lower disc and replace the top. Chill the cake for 30 minutes if the cream seems a bit oozy, and serve dusted with icing sugar, if you like.

Lemon ice

We like to serve this in a hollowed out lemon.

Serves 6

125ml lemon juice
150g caster sugar

a pinch of salt
500ml milk

Heat the lemon juice with the sugar and salt until they dissolve, then remove from the heat and stir in the milk. The milk will curdle, which is unsightly for now but harmless. Check the balance of acidity and sweetness and adjust if necessary. Churn the mixture in an ice-cream machine until frozen – the result will be somewhere between a milky sorbet and a very light ice cream.

Oloroso cream with berries and almonds

This pudding is a Spanish version of zabaglione, made with oloroso sherry instead of Marsala wine.

Serves 6

8 large organic egg yolks, at room temperature
grated zest of 1 lemon
150g caster sugar

5 grates of nutmeg (optional)
200ml medium oloroso sherry
400ml whipping cream

To serve

500g strawberries, cut into quarters, or 400g raspberries or blackberries
25g caster sugar

grated zest of 1 lemon
50g slivered almonds, toasted and dusted with icing sugar

First combine the egg yolks, lemon zest, sugar and nutmeg in a large bowl and place on top of a saucepan of simmering water, making sure the water doesn't touch the base of the bowl. Using a balloon whisk, whip vigorously until the mixture is very thick and quite hot. Wait until it is so thick that you fear it might start to catch at the bottom of the bowl, then start adding the oloroso, about a tablespoonful at a time, still whisking away. Wait for the mixture to thicken after each addition of the sherry.

Transfer to a clean bowl, cover with cling film and leave to cool, then chill for an hour or two in the fridge. Whip the cream and fold it into the sabayon. Spoon into individual glasses or a large serving bowl and refrigerate for at least 2 hours, until set.

About 10 minutes before serving, combine the berries with the sugar and lemon zest and leave to macerate. Serve the mousse with the berries and a scattering of toasted almonds.

Apple purée with crème fraîche and caramel

We are lucky enough to have an apple tree on the allotment and one in our garden. We end up eating a lot of puréed apple, and this recipe is our favourite combination. The caramel gives an extra bitter-crunch excitement, but if you don't want to make it, muscovado sugar tastes wonderful sprinkled on top.

Serves 4

1kg apples (preferably a 50/50 mixture of cooking apples and eating apples such as Granny Smith or Jonagold) or pears, peeled, cored and cut into chunks

250g caster sugar (more if the fruit is very tart)
4cm piece of cinnamon stick
500ml water
15g unsalted butter

To serve

100g caster sugar
1 tablespoon water

200ml crème fraîche

Put the fruit, sugar, cinnamon and water in a saucepan and simmer for about 15 minutes, until the fruit breaks down. Depending on the variety and ripeness of the fruit, it may take a little longer, and may need a bit more sugar. Remove the cinnamon stick, stir in the butter until melted and leave to cool. Chill the purée, then mash it if any lumps remain.

When you are ready to serve, put the 100g sugar in a small, heavy-based saucepan and moisten with the water. Heat gently until the sugar has dissolved, then raise the heat and boil, swirling the pan gently – do not stir it – until you have a golden-brown caramel. Remove from the heat immediately (it will continue to darken), quenching the pan by immersing the base in cold water if it looks as if it's going too dark.

Spoon the apple compôte into shallow serving bowls, spread it flat and put a dollop of crème fraîche in the centre of each. When the caramel has thickened to the texture of runny honey, drizzle it over each portion. Use a dessertspoon held high over the bowl to do this, waving it to produce a dense mesh of thin strands of caramel on the surface of the fruit and cream. Leave for a minute to harden, then serve.

Yoghurt with tahini and honey

Sometimes the simplest things are best. This dish makes a great breakfast, or a quick and easy dessert.

Serves 4

500g good-quality Greek yoghurt,
    such as Total
5 tablespoons tahini
5 tablespoons runny honey (the better
    the honey, the better the finished dish)

Put the yoghurt into a serving bowl. Stir the tahini and honey together to make a smooth paste, then drizzle this on to the yoghurt. Run a spoon or skewer through the yoghurt, tahini and honey mixture to produce a marbled effect and the dish is ready to serve.

Pumpkin ensaimadas

Ensaimadas, the airy, spiralled yeast pastries from Mallorca, have become famous across Spain. While you will find plain ensaimadas in almost any Spanish bakery, the favourite Mallorquí ones are stuffed with *crema* (custard) or *cabello de ángel* ('angel's hair' – sweetened spaghetti squash). This is a version of the *cabello de ángel* filling, substituting grated kabocha squash for the hard-to-find spaghetti squash. If you'd rather make *crema* ensaimadas, just make the crème pâtissière from the Pine Nut and Rosewater Tropézienne (see page 291), omitting the rosewater and whipped cream, and use it in place of the pumpkin. The pastries taste so good warm from the oven they will make you want to cry, but be sure to let them cool for 15 minutes, as the filling gets painfully hot. Warm them gently for a few minutes if they go cold.

Makes 8

450g plain flour

$1^1/_2$ teaspoons dried yeast

150ml tepid water

2 organic eggs

1 organic egg yolk

$^1/_2$ teaspoon fine sea salt

75g caster sugar

2 tablespoons extra virgin olive oil,
   plus extra for forming the pastries

80g lard (or butter), softened at room
   temperature

icing sugar for dusting

Pumpkin filling

400g kabocha squash, grated (about
   700g whole squash, peeled, seeded
   and grated with a cheese grater)

250g caster sugar

juice of 1 lemon

$^1/_2$ teaspoon ground cinnamon

Mix 100g of the flour with the yeast and water and leave until foamy and doubled in bulk. Now add the remaining flour, the eggs, egg yolk, salt, sugar and oil and knead to a smooth dough (this is easiest in a mixer fitted with a dough hook). Leave to rise, covered, for about 2 hours, until at least doubled in bulk.

Meanwhile, make the filling. Combine all the ingredients and simmer over a medium heat for 15–20 minutes, until jammy. Cool to room temperature before using.

Have ready 2 oiled baking sheets and a metal or plastic tray on which to form the pastries. Pour a puddle of oil on the tray, to keep the dough from sticking to your hands or the work surface. Divide the dough into 8 balls without kneading it too much. Put one ball on the oily tray and use your fingers to press and pull it to a thin oval, about 20–25cm long by 15cm wide. Spread a dollop of lard over the surface, then arrange about an eighth of the pumpkin filling in a thin sausage along a long edge of the dough. Roll it up into a tight cigarette, taking care not to tear the dough, then coil it up, like a Danish pastry, tucking the end under to prevent it unrolling. Put the ensaimada on one of your baking sheets while you make the rest. It should be quite oily on the outside, which will prevent it drying out as it rises. Leave to rise at room temperature for 2–3 hours, until doubled in bulk.

Preheat the oven to 200°C/400°F/Gas 6. Bake the pastries for 15 minutes, until fully risen, golden and aromatic. Dust with plenty of icing sugar when hot from the oven and transfer to a wire rack to cool until safe to eat.

Quince sorbet

Serves 6–8

4 medium quinces (about 800g)
350g caster sugar
1 vanilla pod

$^1/_2$ bottle (375ml) of white wine
400ml water
juice of $^1/_2$ lemon

Wash the quinces and, if they are furry ones, rub off the fur under running water. Place the whole quinces in a pan with the sugar, vanilla pod and wine. Cover with foil and a tight-fitting lid and simmer gently on a very low heat for 3–3$^1/_2$ hours, until they're really soft and a burnt-orange colour. Push the mixture through a sturdy fine sieve, or a mouli, while still warm. Sieve again if the texture of the puréed quince is still too gritty. Stir in the water and lemon juice and leave to cool completely. Place in an ice-cream machine and freeze according to the manufacturer's instructions.

Quince jelly

Serves 6

3 medium quinces (about 600g)
juice of 1 lemon
200g caster sugar

4cm piece of cinnamon stick
1 litre water
16g leaf gelatine

Peel the quinces and, with a sharp knife, cut each one into 8 long wedges and cut the core from each wedge. Toss them in the lemon juice as you go, to keep them from going brown. When all are done, put them in a saucepan with the sugar, cinnamon and water, cover with a tight-fitting lid and simmer on the lowest heat for 2$^1/_2$ hours, until the liquid is a rosy pink. Using a slotted spoon, gently lift the wedges into a jelly mould (a bowl will do fine), leaving all the liquid behind. Strain it and measure out 800ml, discarding any left over. Soak the gelatine in cold water for 3 minutes, until soft. Squeeze dry and stir it into the hot syrup until completely melted. Pour the syrup over the quince and leave to cool, then refrigerate overnight. Stand the mould in hot water for a few seconds before you turn this delicate, fragrant jelly out on to a plate.

Orange jelly

Serves 4

75g caster sugar

450ml fresh orange juice (squeeze the oranges by hand)

8g leaf gelatine

1 tablespoon orange blossom water

1 teaspoon grated orange zest, blanched briefly to remove any bitterness

1 orange, peeled and segmented with a knife to remove all tough membranes

Warm the sugar in the orange juice until dissolved and steaming (but not boiling). Remove from the heat. Soak the gelatine in cold water for 3 minutes, until soft, then squeeze it dry and stir it into the hot juice until completely melted. Stir in the orange blossom water. Pour into a jelly mould or bowl and leave to cool, then refrigerate for a few hours until just starting to thicken. Stir in the orange zest and segments and return to the fridge to set – preferably overnight. Stand the mould in hot water for a few seconds before you turn the jelly out on to a plate.

Pomegranate jelly

Serves 4

75g caster sugar

450ml fresh pomegranate juice (see page 52 – you will need the seeds of about $4^1/_2$ pomegranates) or use Pom (pomegranate juice from concentrate)

9g leaf gelatine

70g fresh pomegranate seeds (the seeds of $^1/_2$ pomegranate)

Warm the sugar in the pomegranate juice until dissolved and steaming (but not boiling). Soak the gelatine in cold water for 3 minutes, until soft. Squeeze it dry and stir it into the hot juice until completely melted. Pour into a jelly mould or bowl and leave to cool, then refrigerate for a few hours until starting to thicken. Stir in the whole pomegranate seeds and return to the fridge to set – preferably overnight. Stand the mould in hot water for a few seconds before you turn this rich, purple jelly out on to a plate.

Clockwise from top: chocolate ice cream, quince sorbet, lemon ice, saffron ice cream, cherry and anis sorbet, and in the centre, mango ice cream.

Saffron ice cream with pistachio biscuits

One of our old chefs, Rodrigo Grossmann, now cooks at my brother's hotel, the George in Rye, where he makes a delicious saffron ice cream that inspired us to have a go.

Serves 6–8

285ml milk

300ml double cream

5cm piece of cinnamon stick

$1/2$ tablespoon green cardamom pods

50g caster sugar

200ml evaporated milk

200ml sweetened condensed milk

a smallish pinch (about 20 strands) of saffron, soaked in 1 tablespoon boiling water

Pistachio biscuits (makes about 40)

220g unsalted pistachios, shelled

100g blanched almonds

125g caster sugar

a pinch of ground cinnamon or cardamom

25g plain flour

2 organic eggs

Bring the milk, cream, cinnamon and cardamom to the boil and simmer for 20 minutes to infuse the mixture and reduce it by about a quarter. Stir in the sugar and remove from the heat. Leave to cool and infuse for about an hour.

Strain out the spices, then stir in the evaporated milk, the condensed milk and the saffron water. Churn in an ice-cream machine until set, then transfer to the freezer to firm up.

Preheat the oven to 190°C/375°F/Gas 5. For the biscuits, put 170g of the pistachios in a food processor with the almonds, 100g of the sugar, the spice and flour and whizz until fine. Add the eggs and pulse until incorporated. Mix the remaining pistachios and sugar with $1^1/2$ teaspoons of water and set aside.

Line a baking tray with a silicone sheet or baking parchment. Use 2 teaspoons to dollop pieces of the dough, the size of a large marble, on the sheet, leaving a little room between them. Moisten your finger and make a small well in the centre of each biscuit. Place 3 or 4 of the sugar-coated pistachios in the centre of each and bake for 10 minutes, until starting to turn golden at the edges. Leave to cool completely before eating.

Pomegranate granizado

Serves 4

100g caster sugar

2 tablespoons runny honey

450ml fresh pomegranate juice (see page 52 – you will need the seeds of about 4$^1/_2$ pomegranates) or use Pom (pomegranate juice from concentrate)

1 teaspoon rosewater

70g fresh pomegranate seeds (the seeds of $^1/_2$ a pomegranate), frozen

a few mint leaves (optional)

Combine the sugar, honey, pomegranate juice and rosewater and stir until the sugar is completely dissolved. Transfer to a baking dish, place in the freezer and stir every 20–30 minutes with a fork as it freezes, to produce blood-red crystals of fragrant ice. Serve with the frozen seeds and, perhaps, a few mint leaves strewn on top.

Chocolate-orange torte

Serves 6

125ml orange juice

grated zest of $^1/_2$ large orange

100g caster sugar

125g unsalted butter, at room temperature, diced

200g best-quality dark chocolate (70 per cent cocoa solids), broken into chunks

3 organic eggs

Preheat the oven to 160°C/325°F/Gas 3. Butter a 20cm solid cake tin and line the base and sides with baking parchment.

Put the orange juice, zest and sugar in a small saucepan and bring to the boil. Put the butter and chocolate in a bowl, pour over the boiling juice and stir until melted – there should be just enough heat in the liquid to melt the solids, but you may have to heat the bowl briefly by placing it over a saucepan of hot water. Beat the eggs by hand until well mixed but not frothy, then add the melted chocolate mixture and stir with the whisk until incorporated. Pour into the cake tin and bake for 30–35 minutes, until a tiny bit wobbly. Remove from the oven, leave to cool to room temperature, then refrigerate to set the cake. Turn it out carefully.

Chocolate ice cream

Serves 4

500ml milk
50g cocoa powder
8cm piece of cinnamon stick
    or 1 level teaspoon crushed
    cardamom seeds
4 large organic egg yolks

125g caster sugar
150g best-quality dark chocolate (70
    per cent cocoa solids), broken into
    chunks

Stir a little of the milk into the cocoa powder to make a thick paste, then slowly add the remaining milk (this is to avoid lumps). Transfer to a saucepan, add the cinnamon or cardamom and bring to the boil. Take the pan off the heat and leave to infuse for 10 minutes.

    Beat the egg yolks with the sugar, then slowly add the hot milk to the yolks, stirring with a whisk to prevent curdling. Return the mixture to the pan and cook over a medium heat, stirring constantly with a wooden spoon, until it starts to thicken (it should coat the back of the spoon). Remove from the heat and strain into a bowl. Add the chocolate, leave for a few minutes to melt in the hot custard, then stir to incorporate. Lay a sheet of cling film directly on the surface to prevent a skin forming and leave to cool, then freeze in an ice-cream machine.

Marzeh's vermicelli pudding

Marzeh is the mother of a school friend. She cooks the most wonderful Pakistani and Iranian food. Many simple influences have filtered through to the Moro kitchen from her. This simple, sensual and refreshing pudding made a huge impression on me (Samuel) the first time I ate it. It was so yummy! It was also the first time I had rosewater.

Serves 6

25g unsalted butter (clarified butter or ghee is best)

100g vermicelli nests, broken up with your hands

650ml milk

200ml evaporated milk

100g caster sugar

$1/_2$ teaspoon ground cardamom

2 teaspoons rosewater

25g shelled raw pistachios, chopped

Melt the butter over a medium heat, then add the vermicelli and fry for about 10 minutes, until browned. Be sure to stir constantly, lest they burn in the corners of the pan. Add the milk, evaporated milk, sugar and cardamom and simmer for 10 minutes or until the vermicelli are cooked. Leave to cool, stir in the rosewater, then refrigerate – the mixture will thicken to a spooning consistency. If it thickens to a solid mass, just stir in a little milk to loosen it. Serve chilled, with the chopped pistachios scattered on top.

Moro plates

Here are a few main course plates that give an idea of how we eat at home and in the restaurant. The combinations take into account the seasons, the culture, textures and tastes. At Moro, when simply cooking chicken, lamb or beef, they are always marinated (see pages 236–7).

SPRING
- Chicken/lamb/fish with spring vegetable pilav (page 158) with seasoned yoghurt and a green salad with a lemon dressing.
- Lamb, beef, chicken/pork with artichokes and potatoes with oloroso served with watercress/rocket salad with sherry vinegar dressing.
- Lamb/chicken/fish with beetroot and broad bean salad (page 124) served with boiled potatoes or dressed lentils.

SUMMER
- Simply cooked fish/chicken/lamb with braised celery with tomatoes, olives and coriander (page 175) accompanied by spinach fried with olive oil and a little garlic in a wok.
- Simply cooked chicken or fish with fried aubergines with salmorejo sauce (page 262) served with lentils dressed with olive oil, mint and parsley.
- Chicken/fish with courgettes with almonds (page 164) with seasoned yoghurt.

AUTUMN
- Chicken/pork/beef/game with piquillo peppers with thyme and crispy potatoes (pages 162 and 186) with simply cooked cabbage/greens or water cress salad with sherry vinegar dressing.
- Pork/lamb/beef/chicken with pumpkin pisto (page 189) and green salad with sherry vinegar dressing.
- Fish/chicken/lamb/beef/pork, seared mushrooms (page 63) with roast or boiled potatoes sprinkled with a little smoked paprika.

WINTER
- Chicken/lamb/fish with okra with pomegranates and yoghurt (page 178).
- Pork/chicken with Trinxat (page 196) and a bitter salad with sherry vinegar dressing.
- Lamb/chicken/fish, cabbage and bulgur wheat pilav and beetroot salad with pistachio sauce (pages 198 and 144) served with a wedge of lemon or seasoned yoghurt on the side.

Index

Page numbers in **bold** denote an illustration